Ron Paul Speaks

Ron Paul Speaks

Compiled and edited by
Philip Haddad and Roger Marsh

Introduction by Ron Paul

The Lyons Press
Guilford, Connecticut
An imprint of The Globe Pequot Press

The Lyons Press is an imprint of The Globe Pequot Press.

Cover photos: Ron Paul 2008
Cover design: Georgiana Goodwin
Text design: Sheryl P. Kober

Library of Congress Cataloging-in-Publication Data
is available on file.

ISBN 978-1-59921-448-1

Printed in the United States of America

10 9 8 7 6 5 4 3 2 1

We find it most appropriate to dedicate this project to Ron Paul.

Contents

Who is Ron Paul?

"We should not trick ourselves into believing that we can pick and choose which part of the Bill of Rights we support."

–Ron Paul

How did Ron Paul go from the presidential candidate with the second lowest name recognition to an Internet sensation–inspiring an explosion of grassroots activity across the country?

Texas Congressman Ronald Ernest Paul may be best known for his no-compromise stand on the U.S. Constitution and his love for the principles of the founding fathers–a lean federal government and a noninterventionist foreign policy. In Congress, he earned the nickname Dr. No, as he does not vote for any legislation unless it is authorized by the Constitution, and he is a medical doctor.

Paul believes in Austrian school economics and opposes fiat increases to money in circulation. He is the only 2008 presidential candidate who voted against the Iraq War Resolution in 2002. He wants to withdraw from the UN and NATO to allow strong national sovereignty. He advocates free trade. He supports tight border control and disagrees with providing welfare for illegal aliens.

Ron Paul follows the Constitution and votes against all proposals for new government spending, initiatives, or taxes. In fact, he would abolish the federal income tax system and scale federal spending back to where it was in the year 2000. Instead of taxing personal income, he would fund the federal government through excise taxes and uniform non-protectionist tariffs.

Paul considers many federal agencies unnecessary bureaucracies and would eliminate them. He has been described as a conservative, a Constitutionalist, and a Libertarian.

Ron Paul was born August 20, 1923, in Green Tree, Pennsylvania (near Pittsburgh), the son of Howard Caspar Paul and Margaret "Peggy" Paul. Howard was the son of a German immigrant with an eighth-grade education who owned the Green Tree Dairy with his brothers, Lewis and Arthur. Ron Paul excelled in track and field at Dormont High School, and was offered a full scholarship in track at a major university upon graduation in 1953, but turned it down. He feared surgery from a knee injury might get in the way, and instead, he paid his own way through his first year at Gettysburg College with money he saved from delivering newspapers, selling lemonade, and mowing lawns.

He graduated from Gettysburg College in 1957 and married his high school sweetheart, Carol Wells, the same year. He graduated from Duke University School of Medicine in 1961 and served as a flight surgeon in the U.S. Air Force during the 1960s. The couple moved to Texas in 1968, and he began his medical practice in Brazoria County. As an obstetrician/gynecologist, Dr. Paul has delivered more than four thousand babies over his forty-year medical practice. The Pauls currently resides in Lake Jackson, Texas, and are the parents of five children, seventeen grandchildren, and one great grandchild.

Early in Paul's career, he was influenced by the writings of Friedrich Hayek's *Road to Serfdom* and the works of Ayn Rand and Ludwig von Mises. He credits economists Hans Sennholz and Murray Rothbard with his fascination for economics. President Richard Nixon closed the "gold window" August 15, 1971, when the U.S. dollar departed from the gold standard. Dr. Paul decided to enter politics that day, reflecting later,

"After that day, all money would be political money rather than money of real value. I was astounded."

Paul has represented Texas districts in the U.S. House of Representatives during 1976–1977, 1979–1985, and 1997 to the present. He ran for president in 1988 as an independent and Libertarian nominee and placed third in the popular vote.

In Congress, Paul has never voted to increase taxes. He has never voted for an unbalanced budget. He has never voted for a federal restriction on gun ownership. He has never voted to raise congressional pay. He has never taken a government-paid junket. He has never voted to increase the power of the executive branch. He voted against the Patriot Act. He voted against regulating the Internet. He voted against the Iraq war. He does not participate in the lucrative congressional pension program. He returns a portion of his annual congressional office budget to the U.S. Treasury every year.

Paul has introduced many bills in Congress that apply to tax relief for the entire country. Some of the many notable bills are the Teacher Tax Cut Act, the Professional Educators Tax Relief Act, and the Education Improvement Tax Cut Act. These bills offer either tax credit, cuts, or incentives for donations toward scholarships.

Protecting constitutional liberties is a top priority for Paul, who introduced the American Freedom Agenda Act of 2007. In part, it requires that federal intelligence gathering is conducted in accordance with the Foreign Intelligence Surveillance Act (FISA). It creates a mechanism for challenging presidential signing statements, repeals the Military Commissions Act, and prohibits kidnapping, detentions, and torture abroad. It also protects journalists who publish information received from the executive branch.

Paul is concerned that individual congressmen are voting on lengthy pieces of legislation before actually reading the bills, such as the Patriot Act, which numbered more than three hundred pages and was enacted into law less than twenty-four hours after being introduced. Paul has proposed "Sunlight Rule" legislation with the intent of giving lawmakers sufficient time to read bills before voting on them.

He sponsored successful legislation to prevent the Department of Housing and Urban Development from seizing a church in New York through eminent domain. By successfully amending other legislation, he also barred American participation in any UN "global tax."

The U.S. Gold Commission created by Congress in 1982 was Paul's and Jesse Helms's vision, and Paul's conclusions from the commission were published by the Cato Institute as a book, *The Case for Gold.* It is currently available from the Mises Institute, of which Paul is a distinguished counselor.

One of the many interesting things about Paul is his impact on citizens engaging in the political process. As one of six Republicans to vote against the Iraq War Resolution, Paul inspired the funding of a group called the National Peace Lobby Project to promote a resolution he cosponsored to repeal the war.

Paul serves on the House Foreign Affairs Committee (having been on the Western Hemisphere and the Asian and Pacific subcommittees); the Joint Economic Committee; and the Committee on Financial Services (as Ranking Member of the Domestic and International Monetary Policy, Trade and Technology subcommittee); and is Vice Chair of the Oversight and Investigations subcommittee.

Paul served as honorary chair of the Republican Liberty Caucus. He also hosts a luncheon every Thursday for the Liberty Committee, a group designed to bring together liberty-minded representatives from both sides of the aisle. He is a founding member of the

Congressional Rural Caucus and the Congressional Wildlife Refuge Caucus.

Throughout the years of being a congressman, Paul has picked up faithful supporters who appreciate the straightforward Constitutionalist. An overwhelming majority of his campaign contributions come from individuals. In 2005 and 2006, individuals contributed 96.8 percent of the funds he raised. Many awards and honors have been bestowed on Paul during his career in Congress, from organizations such as the National Taxpayers Union, Citizens Against Government Waste, the Council for a Competitive Economy, Young Americans for Freedom, and countless others.

Paul promotes many issues that apply to people of varied backgrounds, such as limited government, low taxes, free markets, a return to sound monetary policy, ending the war in Iraq, and pursuing foreign policy that helps to ensure friendships with other countries.

A vocal opponent to inflation, Paul argues that the long-term erosion of the dollar's purchasing power arises from its lack of commodity backing, which would restrain excess "printing" of money and consequent devaluation. He would push to legalize gold and silver as legal tender and remove the sales tax on them, so that gold-backed notes and digital gold currencies can compete on a level playing field with fiat Federal Reserve notes, allowing individuals a choice whether to use "sound money" to protect their purchasing power or to continue using fiat money.

Paul remains a top Internet search term as ranked by Technorati. With enormous popularity on the Internet, he has the highest amount of subscribers on YouTube pertaining to all of the presidential candidates.

A true grassroots movement is very motivated to get out the word on Paul's message. Throughout his 2008 presidential campaign, he has been a leading candidate in Republican straw polls.

It has been very inspiring to watch a diverse group of people across the nation rally behind an ideal more than a candidate.

It started with a Web site that was not updated for many months–RonPaulExplore.com–and many waited with baited breath. Could it be true that the number-one modern statesman would again run for president, this time under a major party wherein the system wouldn't be quite so biased?

Then an explosion happened that even took Paul by surprise.

Every quarter he raised more money and support, setting a Republican fund-raising record for a twenty-four-hour period. Remarkable indeed for an ordinarily soft-spoken congressman whose words have not changed over the years and who was not that well known, aside from those that took an interest in smaller government, noninterventionism, freedom, and prosperity.

Paul's supporters have harnessed the Internet quite well, with giant leaps in fund-raising and outreach from blogs to social networking sites. On December 16, 2007, he had the largest one-day fund-raiser in U.S. political history, garnering over $6 million in twenty-four hours through an effort largely independent of the campaign. Paul won almost every Internet presidential debate poll, numerous straw polls across the country, and gathered support from diverse cross sections of America. We have never seen such an increase in output from varied sections of America rallying behind a presidential candidate in a major party.

Some have remarked that Dr. Paul cured their apathy. Paul responded that they had cured his skepticism.

America is watching a candidate that has renewed optimism in the voting public. You can have an impact.

There can once again be a government "by the people and for the people." There may very well be new records and legacies set by this movement, and we are honored to be a small part of it by providing a collection of timeless wisdom on numerous topics.

Special thanks to our editors at The Globe Pequot Press, Gary Krebs and Kaleena Cote; and our literary agent, Jeff Herman and The Jeff Herman Agency, LLC.

In August 2007, we saw firsthand how the words Ron Paul speaks consistently over time can move a crowd. We stood on the media platform at the Pittsburgh area rally in Mars, Pennsylvania, and videotaped Paul's address. Afterwards, we interviewed Ron Paul on camera as well as his son, Ronnie Jr.; Campaign Manager Lew Moore; and Communications Director Jesse Benton. Our YouTube.com/tremontavenue uploads have received thousands of hits.

Philip took a closer look and personally campaigned for Ron Paul in New Hampshire, Wisconsin, Illinois, and Pennsylvania–walking door-to-door with literature, street sign-waving, and helping to man phone banks to get the word out. He was able to meet many people from around the country–and the world–who were coming together with personal funds to take their support into the streets and homes of America. The spirit of Ron Paul supporters is thriving and seems poised to go beyond the 2008 election as the Ron Paul Revolution.

What is next is anyone's guess, but indications point to a groundswell of civic activity based on what made this country great.

Philip Haddad
Scottdale, PA

Roger Marsh
Chicago, IL

Introduction by Ron Paul

> **" . . . man is not free unless government is limited. There's a clear cause and effect here that is as neat and predictable as a law of physics: As government expands, liberty contracts."**
>
> **–Ronald Reagan**

We've all heard the words "democracy" and "freedom" used countless times, especially in the context of our invasion of Iraq. They are used interchangeably in modern political discourse, yet their true meanings are very different.

George Orwell wrote about "meaningless words" that are endlessly repeated in the political arena*. Words like "freedom," "democracy," and "justice," Orwell explained, have been abused so long that their original meanings have been eviscerated. In Orwell's view, political words were "often used in a

**Politics and the English Language*, 1946.

consciously dishonest way." Without precise meanings behind words, politicians and elites can obscure reality and condition people to reflexively associate certain words with positive or negative perceptions. In other words, unpleasant facts can be hidden behind purposely meaningless language. As a result, Americans have been conditioned to accept the word "democracy" as a synonym for freedom, and thus to believe that democracy is unquestionably good.

The problem is that democracy is not freedom. Democracy is simply majoritarianism, which is inherently incompatible with real freedom. Our founding fathers clearly understood this, as evidenced not only by our *republican* constitutional system, but also by their writings in the *Federalist Papers* and elsewhere. James Madison cautioned that under a democratic government, "There is nothing to check the inducement to sacrifice the weaker party or the obnoxious individual." John Adams argued that democracies merely grant revocable rights to citizens depending on the whims of the masses, while a republic exists to secure and protect preexisting rights. Yet how many Americans know that the word "democracy" is found neither in the Constitution nor the Declaration of Independence, our very founding documents?

A truly democratic election in Iraq, without U.S. interference and U.S. puppet candidates, almost certainly would result in the creation of a Shiite theocracy. Shiite majority rule in Iraq might well mean the complete political, economic, and social subjugation of the minority Kurd and Sunni Arab populations. Such an outcome would be democratic, but would it be free? Would the Kurds and Sunnis consider themselves free? The administration talks about democracy in Iraq, but is it prepared to accept a democratically elected Iraqi government no matter what its attitude toward the U.S. occupation? Hardly. For all our talk about freedom and democracy, the truth is we have no idea whether Iraqis will be free in the future. They're certainly not free while a foreign army occupies their country. The real test is not whether Iraq adopts a democratic, pro-Western government, but rather whether ordinary Iraqis can lead their personal, religious, social, and business lives without interference from government.

Simply put, freedom is the absence of government coercion. Our founding fathers understood this, and created the least coercive government in the history of the world. The Constitution established a very limited, decentralized government to provide national defense and little else. States, not the federal government, were charged with protecting individuals against criminal force and fraud. For the first time, a government was created solely to protect the rights, liberties, and property of its citizens. Any government coercion beyond that necessary to secure those rights was forbidden, both through the Bill of Rights and the doctrine of strictly enumerated powers. This reflected the founders' belief that democratic government could be as tyrannical as any king.

Few Americans understand that all government action is inherently coercive. If nothing else, government action requires taxes. If taxes were freely paid, they wouldn't be called taxes, they'd be called donations. If we intend to use the word "freedom" in an honest way, we should have the simple integrity to give it real meaning: Freedom is living without government coercion. So when a politician talks about freedom for this group or that, ask yourself whether he is advocating more government action or less.

The political left equates freedom with liberation from material wants, always via a large and benevolent government that exists to create equality on earth. To modern liberals, men are free only when the laws of economics and scarcity are suspended, the landlord is rebuffed, the doctor presents no bill, and groceries are given away. But philosopher Ayn Rand (and many others before her) demolished this argument by explaining how such "freedom" for some is possible only when government takes freedoms away from others. In other words, government claims on the lives and property of those who are expected to provide housing, medical care, food, etc., for others are coercive–and thus incompatible with freedom. "Liberalism," which once stood for civil, political, and economic liberties, has become a synonym for omnipotent coercive government.

The political right equates freedom with national greatness brought about through military strength. Like the left, modern conservatives favor an all-powerful central state–but for militarism, corporatism, and faith-based welfarism. Unlike the Taft-Goldwater conservatives of yesteryear, today's Republicans are eager to expand government spending, increase the federal police apparatus, and intervene militarily around the world. The last tenuous links between conservatives and support for smaller government have been severed. "Conservatism," which once meant respect for tradition and distrust of active government, has transformed into big government utopian grandiosity.

Orwell certainly was right about the use of meaningless words in politics. If we hope to remain free, we must cut through the fog and attach concrete meanings to the words politicians use to deceive us. We must reassert that America is a republic, not a democracy, and remind ourselves that the Constitution places limits on government that no majority can overrule. We must resist any use of the word "freedom" to describe state action. We must reject the current meaningless designations of "liberals" and "conservatives," in favor of an accurate term for both: statists.

Every politician on earth claims to support freedom. The problem is so few of them understand the simple meaning of the word.

Ron Paul
Speaks

★ 2004 Election ★

The biggest difference involved their views on moral and family values. It was evident that the views regarding gay marriage and abortion held by Senator Kerry did not sit well with a majority of American voters, who were then motivated to let their views be known through their support for President Bush. This contributed to the "mandate" the president received more than any other issue. But it begs the question: If the mandate given was motivated by views held on moral values, does the president get carte blanche on all the other programs that are much less conservative? It appears the president and his neocon advisors assume the answer is yes.[1]

More people voted for President Bush than any other presidential candidate in our history. And because of the turnout, more people voted against an incumbent president than ever before. However, President Bush was

reelected by the narrowest popular vote margin of any incumbent president since Woodrow Wilson in 1916. The numbers are important and measurable; the long-term results are less predictable. The president and many others have said these results give the president a "mandate." Exactly what that means and what it may lead to is of great importance to us all. Remember, the nation reelected a president in 1972 with a much bigger mandate who never got a chance to use his political capital.[2]

More important was the reaction of the international exchange markets immediately following the election. The dollar took a dive and gold rose. This indicated that holders of the trillions of dollars slushing around the world interpreted the results to mean that even with conservatives in charge, unbridled spending will not decrease and will actually grow. They also expect the current account deficit and our national debt to increase. This means the economic consequence of continuing our risky fiscal and monetary policy is something Congress should be a lot more concerned about. One Merrill Lynch money manager responded to the election by saying, "Bush getting reelected means a bigger deficit, a weaker dollar, and higher gold prices." Another broker added, **"Four more years of Bush is a gift to the gold markets—more war, more deficits, more division."** [3]

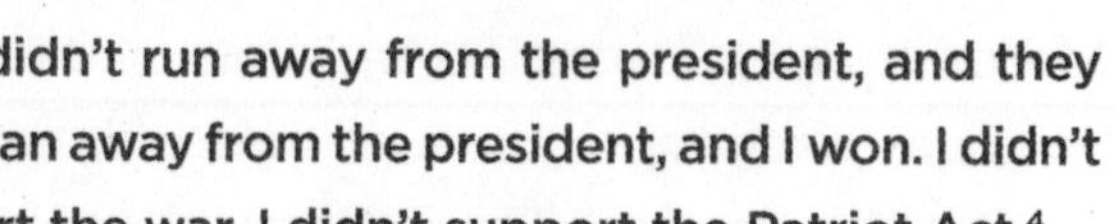

★ 2006 Election ★

They didn't run away from the president, and they lost; I ran away from the president, and I won. I didn't support the war. I didn't support the Patriot Act.[4]

★ Abortion ★

If you don't protect life, you can't protect liberty. And we now are at a stage where we allow the national government through the Supreme

Court to permit the killing of an unborn baby anytime before birth.[5]

Though abortion is now an ingrained part of our society, the moral conflict over the issue continues to rage **with no end in sight.**[6]

In the 1960s, as part of the new age of permissiveness, people's attitudes changed regarding abortion. This led to a change in the law as reflected in court rulings—especially Roe vs. Wade. **The people's moral standards changed first, followed by the laws. It was not the law or the Supreme Court that brought on the age of abortion.** I've wondered if our casual acceptance of the deaths inflicted on both sides in the Vietnam War, and its association with the drug culture that many used to blot out the tragic human losses, contributed to the cheapening of preborn human life and the acceptance of abortion as a routine and acceptable practice.[7]

It is imperative that we resolve the dilemma of why it's proper to financially reward an abortionist who acts one minute before birth, yet we arrest and prosecute a new mother who throws her child into a garbage bin one minute after birth.[8]

★ Accountability ★

Mr. Speaker, Supreme Court Justice Louis Brandeis famously said, "Sunlight is the best disinfectant." In order to shine sunlight on the practices of the House of Representatives, and thus restore public trust and integrity to this institution, I am introducing the "Sunlight Rule." This measure amends House rules to ensure members have adequate time to study a bill before being asked to vote on it. One of the chief causes of increasing

public cynicism is the way major pieces of legislation are brought to the floor without members having an opportunity to read the bills.[9]

For example, just this past December the House voted on the fiscal year 2006 Defense Appropriations conference report at approximately 4:00 a.m.—just four hours after the report was filed. Yet the report contained language dealing with avian flu, including controversial language regarding immunity liability for vaccine manufacturers, that was added in the House–Senate conference on the bill. Considering legislation on important issues in this manner is a dereliction of our duty as the people's elected representatives.[10]

My proposed rule requires that no piece of legislation, including conference reports, can be brought before the House of Representatives unless it has been available to members and staff both in print and electronic versions for at least ten days. My bill also requires that a manager's amendment making substantive changes to a bill be available in both printed and electronic forms at least seventy-two hours before a vote.[11]

The Sunlight Rule provides the American people the opportunity to be involved in enforcing congressional rules by allowing citizens to move for censure of any representative who votes for a bill brought to the floor in violation of this act. The Sunlight Rule can never be waived by the Rules Committee or House leadership.[12]

★ Afghanistan ★

The obvious shortcomings of our regime change and occupation of Afghanistan are now readily apparent. The Taliban was ousted from power, but they have regrouped and

threaten the delicate stability that now exists in that country. Opium drug production is once again a major operation, with drug lords controlling a huge area of the country outside Kabul. And now the real nature of the government we created has been revealed in the case of Abdul Rahman, the Muslim who faced a possible death sentence from the Karzai administration for converting to Christianity. Even now that Mr. Rahman is free due to Western pressure, his life remains in danger.[15]

It has been known for years that Unocal, a U.S. company, has been anxious to build a pipeline through northern Afghanistan, but it has not been possible due to the weak Afghan central government. We should not be surprised now that many contend that the plan for the UN to "nation build" in Afghanistan is a logical and important consequence of this desire. **The crisis has merely given those interested in this project an excuse to replace the government of Afghanistan.** Since we don't even know if bin Laden is in Afghanistan, and since other countries are equally supportive of him, our concentration on this Taliban "target" remains suspect by many.[14]

Unbelievably, to this day our foreign aid continues to flow into Afghanistan, even as we prepare to go to war against her. My suggestion is, **not only should we stop this aid immediately, but we should never have started it in the first place.**[15]

Our foolish funding of Afghan terrorists hardly ended in the 1980s, however. Millions of your tax dollars continue to pour into Afghanistan even today. Our government publicly supported the Taliban right up until September 11. Already in 2001 the United States has provided $125 million in so-called humanitarian aid to the country, making us the world's single largest donor to Afghanistan. Rest assured the money went straight to the Taliban, and not to the impoverished, starving residents that make up most of the popula-

tion. Do we really expect a government as intolerant and anti-West as the Taliban to use our foreign aid for humane purposes? If so, we are incredibly naive; if not, we foolishly have been seeking to influence a government that regards America as an enemy.[16]

Incredibly, in May the United States announced that we would reward the Taliban with an additional $43 million in aid for its actions in banning the cultivation of poppy used to produce heroin and opium. Taliban rulers had agreed to assist us in our senseless drug war by declaring opium growing "against the will of God." They weren't serious, of course. Although reliable economic data for Afghanistan is nearly impossible to find (there simply is not much of an economy), the reality is that opium is far and away the most profitable industry in the country. The Taliban was hardly prepared to give up virtually its only source of export revenue, any more than the demand for opium was suddenly going to disappear. If anything, Afghanistan's production of opium is growing. Experts estimate it has doubled since 1999; the relatively small country is now believed to provide the raw material for fully 75 percent of the world's heroin. **How tragic that our government was willing to ignore Taliban brutality in its quest to find "victories" in the failed drug war.**[17]

★ Al-Qaeda ★

No evidence existed to show an alliance between Iraq and al-Qaeda before the war, and ironically our presence there is now encouraging al Qaeda and Osama bin Laden to move in to fill the vacuum we created. The only relationship between Iraq and 9/11 is that our policy in the Middle East continues to increase the likelihood of another terrorist attack on our homeland.[18]

Is it not true that northern Iraq, where the administration claimed al-Qaeda were hiding out, is in the control of our "allies," the Kurds?[19]

Is it not true that the vast majority of al-Qaeda leaders who escaped appear to have safely made their way to Pakistan, another of our so-called allies?[20]

Has anyone noticed that Afghanistan is rapidly sinking into total chaos, with bombings and assassinations becoming daily occurrences; and that according to a recent UN report the al-Qaeda "is, by all accounts, alive and well and poised to strike again, how, when, and where it chooses"?[21]

Why are we taking precious military and intelligence resources away from tracking down those who did attack the United States—and who may again attack the United States—and using them to invade countries that have not attacked the United States?[22]

★ Arab League ★

After we left Lebanon in the 1980s, the Arab League was instrumental in brokering an end to that country's fifteen-year civil war. Its chances of helping to stop the fighting in Iraq are far better than depending on the UN, NATO, or the United States. This is a regional dispute that we stirred up but cannot settle. The Arab League needs to assume a lot more responsibility for the mess that our invasion has caused. **We need to get out of the way and let them solve their own problems.**[23]

I would bring our troops home; I would end the war. I would do it rather quickly. [To] anybody who would say, "This would be chaotic," I would say chaos was caused by the fact that we went in there and we've been in for reasons that weren't right or true. It was going in that caused all of the problems. Immediately we could save a

lot of money and save a lot of lives. Those individuals, including the Arab League, would have to settle those problems. I think the Arab League would step in and fill the vacuum.[24]

★ Arctic National Wildlife Refuge (ANWR) ★

One provision of the bill that undeniably would have benefited the American people, the language opening up the ANWR region of Alaska and expanding offshore drilling, was removed from the bill. As my colleagues know, increased gas prices are a top concern of the American people. Expanding the supply of domestically produced oil is an obvious way to address these concerns, yet Congress refuses to take this reasonable step.[25]

I've introduced the Affordable Gas Price Act (HR 2415) to deal with some of these issues. My bill would suspend federal fuel taxes when prices rise above $3 a gallon, giving some immediate relief at the pump.[26]

★ Ballot Access ★

Even candidates able to comply with onerous ballot access rules must devote so many resources to simply getting on the ballot that their ability to communicate ideas to the general public is severely limited.[27]

Perhaps the ballot access laws are one reason why voter turnout has been declining over the past few decades. After all, almost 42 percent of eligible voters have either not registered to vote or have registered as something other than Democrat or Republican.[28]

In order to open up the political process, I have introduced the Voter Freedom Act (HR 1941). HR 1941 establishes uniform standards for ballot access so third-party and independent candidates can at last compete on a level playing field.[29]

★ Bill of Rights ★

At home the war on poverty, terrorism, drugs, or foreign rulers provides an opportunity for authoritarians to rise to power, individuals who think nothing of violating the people's rights to privacy and freedom of speech. They believe their role is to protect the secrecy of government, rather than protect the privacy of citizens. Unfortunately, that is the atmosphere under which we live today, with essentially no respect for the Bill of Rights.[30]

We should not trick ourselves into believing that we can pick and choose which part of the Bill of Rights we support.[31]

The problem with the Bill of Rights is that it restricts the power of the federal government while ensuring maximum liberty for the individual.[32]

One has to raise the question: What's wrong with the existing Bill of Rights, those original Ten Amendments to the Constitution, that a new one must be created to assuage every group, complaint, or situation?[33]

★ Blame Game ★

Since we're not on the verge of mending our ways, the problems will worsen and the blame games will get much more vicious. Shortchanging a large segment of our society

surely will breed conflict that could get out of control. This is a good reason for us to cast aside politics as usual and start finding some reliable answers to our problems.[34]

Sadly, the acrimonious blame game is motivated by the leadership of both parties for the purpose of gaining, or retaining, political power. It doesn't approach a true debate over the wisdom, or lack thereof, of foreign military interventionism and preemptive war.[35]

The blame game is a political event, designed to avoid the serious philosophic debate over our foreign policy of interventionism. The mistakes made by both parties in dragging us into an unwise war are obvious, but the effort to blame one group over the other confuses the real issue. Obviously Congress failed to meet its constitutional obligation regarding war. Debate over prewar intelligence elicits charges of errors, lies, and complicity. It is now argued that those who are critical of the outcome in Iraq are just as much at fault, since they too accepted flawed intelligence when deciding to support the war. This charge is leveled at previous administrations, foreign governments, members of Congress, and the United Nations—all who made the same mistake of blindly accepting the prewar intelligence. Complicity, errors of judgment, and malice are hardly an excuse for such a serious commitment as a preemptive war against a nonexistent enemy.[36]

In spite of the potential problems that may or may not come with our withdrawal, the greater mistake was going in the first place. We need to think more about how to avoid these military encounters, rather than dwelling on the complications that result when we meddle in the affairs of others with no moral or legal authority to do so. **We need less blame game and more reflection about the root cause of our aggressive foreign policy.**[37]

★ Borrowing ★

Thousands of private pension funds are now being dumped on the U.S. government and American taxpayers. We are borrowing over 700 billion dollars each year from foreigners to finance this extravagance, and we now qualify as the greatest international debtor nation in history. Excessive consumption using borrowed money is hardly the way to secure a sound economy.[38]

As a nation dependent on the willingness of foreigners to loan us the money to finance our extravagance, **we now are consuming 80 percent of the world's savings.** Though the Fed does its part in supplying funds by purchasing Treasury debt, foreign central banks and investors have loaned us nearly twice what the Fed has, to the tune of $1.3 trillion. The daily borrowing needed to support our spending habits cannot last.[39]

Borrowing money to cut the deficit is only marginally better than raising taxes. **It may delay the pain for a while, but the cost of government eventually must be paid.**[40]

Federal borrowing means the cost of interest is added, shifting the burden to a different group than those who benefited and possibly even to another generation.[41]

Paying for government spending with Federal Reserve credit, instead of taxing or borrowing from the public, is anything but a good deal for everyone. **In fact it is the most sinister seductive "tax" of them all.** Initially it is unfair to some, but it's dangerous to everyone in the end. It is especially harmful to the middle class, including lower-income working people who are thought not to be paying taxes.[42]

★ Bureaucracy ★

According to some legal experts, at least three-quarters of all federal laws consist of regulations promulgated by federal agencies without the consent, or even the review, of Congress. **Allowing unelected, and thus unaccountable, executive agencies to make law undermines democracy.** Lawmaking by executive agencies also violates the intent of the drafters of the Constitution to separate legislative and executive powers.[43]

Congress's delegation of lawmaking authority to unelected bureaucrats has created a system that seems to owe more to the writings of Franz Kafka than to the writings of James Madison. The volume of regulations promulgated by federal agencies and the constant introduction of new rules makes it impossible for most Americans to know with any certainty the federal laws, regulations, and rules they are required to obey. Thus, almost all

Americans live with the danger that they may be hauled before a federal agency for an infraction they have no reasonable way of knowing is against the law.[44]

While it is easy for members of Congress to complain about out-of-control federal bureaucrats, it was Congress that gave these agencies the ability to create laws.[45]

Today government notoriously interferes with almost every voluntary economic transaction. Consumerism, labor law, wage standards, hiring and firing regulations, political correctness, affirmative action, the Americans with Disabilities Act, the tax code, and others all place a burden on the two parties struggling to transact business.[46]

★ Business ★

Foreign nations could easily criticize the United States for its weak dollar policy, which favors our exporting industries while harming the exporting industries of our trading partners; for our eminent-domain policies, which make a mockery of property rights; and for Sarbanes-Oxley, which unfairly burdens companies operating in this country and causes companies to move to foreign capital markets.[47]

The census also represents a form of corporate welfare, since the personal data collected on hundreds of millions of Americans can be sold to private businesses. Surely business enjoys having such extensive information available from one source, but it's hardly the duty of taxpayers to subsidize the cost of market research.[48]

Envy and power drive both sides–the special interests of big business and the demands of the welfare redistribution crowd.[49]

Today, American businesses, workers, and investors are suffering because Congress was so eager to appear "tough on corporate crime."[50]

★ Central Bankers ★

Officially, our central bankers and our politicians express no fear that the course on which we are set is fraught with great danger to our economy and our political system. The belief that money created out of thin air can work economic miracles, if only properly "managed," is pervasive in D.C.[51]

Alan Greenspan bragged that central bankers in these several decades have gained the knowledge necessary to make paper money respond as if it were gold. **This removes the problem of obtaining gold to back currency, and hence frees politicians from the rigid discipline a gold standard imposes.** Many central bankers in the last fifteen years became so confident they had achieved this milestone that they sold off large hoards of their gold reserves. At other times they tried to prove that paper works better than gold by artificially propping up the dollar by suppressing market gold prices. This recent deception failed just as it did in the 1960s, when our government tried to hold gold artificially low at $35 an ounce. But since they could not truly repeal the economic laws regarding money, just as many central bankers sold, others bought. **It's fascinating that the European central banks sold gold while Asian central banks bought it over the last several years.**[52]

The incentive for central bankers to create new money out of thin air is twofold. One is to practice central economic planning through the manipulation of interest rates. The second is to monetize the escalating federal debt politicians create and thrive on.[53]

In recent years central banks and various financial institutions, all with vested interests in maintaining a workable fiat dollar standard, were not secretive about selling and loaning large amounts of gold to the market even while decreasing gold prices raised serious questions about the wisdom of such a policy. They never admitted to gold price fixing, but the evidence is abundant that they believed if the gold price fell, it would convey a sense of confidence to the market, confidence that they indeed had achieved amazing success in turning paper into gold.[54]

★ Chavez ★

It's become clear the U.S. administration was sympathetic to those who plotted the overthrow of Chavez and was embarrassed by its failure. **The fact that Chavez was democratically elected had little influence on which side we supported.**[55]

U.S. policy supports the overthrow of the democratically elected Chavez government in Venezuela because we don't like the economic policy it pursues.[56]

★ Checks and Balances ★

Unfortunately the legislative branch of our government too often defers to the executive branch,

and offers little resistance to war plans even with no significant threat to our security.[57]

When the issues come before Congress, executive authority is maintained or even strengthened **while real oversight is ignored.**[58]

Finally, why not try something novel, like having Congress act as an independent and equal branch of government? Restore the principle of the separation of powers, so that we can perform our duty to provide checks and balances on an executive branch (and an accommodating judiciary) that spies on Americans, glorifies the welfare state, fights undeclared wars, and enormously increases the national debt. Congress was not meant to be a rubber stamp. It's time for a new direction.[59]

★ China ★

Politicians today fail to realize just how deeply our profligate fiscal and monetary policies of the past three decades have left us in debt to China. **The Chinese government holds over one trillion dollars in reserves, leaving the future of the dollar highly vulnerable to the continued Chinese demand.**[60]

We should remember that losing a war to China over control of North Korea ultimately did not enhance communism in China, as she now has accepted many capitalist principles. In fact, China today outproduces us in many ways—as reflected by our negative trade balance with her.[61]

We also have been careless over the last several years in allowing our military secrets

to find their way into the hands of the Chinese government. At the same time we subsidize trade with China, including sensitive military technology, we also build up the Taiwanese military while continuing to patrol the Chinese border with our spy planes. It's a risky, inconsistent policy.[62]

★ Christianity ★

The sad fact is that even under the despicable rule of Saddam Hussein, Christians were safer in Iraq than they are today. Saddam Hussein's foreign minister was a practicing Christian. Today thousands of Christians have fled Iraq following our occupation, to countries like Jordan and Syria. Those Christians who have remained in Iraq fear for their lives every day. That should tell us something about the shortcomings of a policy that presumes to make the world safe for democracy.[63]

Too often the message from some of our national Christian leaders sounds hateful and decidedly un-Christian in tone. They preach the need for vengeance and war against a country that never attacked nor posed a threat to us. It's just as important to resolve this dilemma as the one involving the abortionist who is paid to kill the unborn while the mother is put in prison for killing her newborn.[64]

★ CIA ★

Considering the CIA's overthrow of Iranian leader Mohammed Mosaddeq in the 1950s, and the CIA's training of the Muhajadin jihadists in Afghanistan in the 1980s, it is entirely possible the actions of the CIA abroad have actually made us less safe and more vulnerable to foreign attack. It would be best to confine our intelligence community to the defense of our territory from foreign attack. This may well mean turning intelligence functions over to the Department of Defense, where they belong.[65]

★

The CIA is what gets us into trouble. I mean, the CIA is what really started things in the Middle East, because the CIA went in and overthrew Mosaddeq in 1953. We put in the shah. The CIA murdered Diem, or participated in the overthrow of the government in Vietnam, which leads to trouble. It's a secret government. Congress has no idea what the CIA is doing, because nobody knows, other than what the CIA is. It is one of the things that is not characteristic of a free society.[66]

★

Osama bin Laden, a wealthy man, left Saudi Arabia in 1979 to join American-sponsored so-called freedom fighters in Afghanistan. He received financial assistance, weapons, and training from our CIA, just as his allies in Kosovo continue to receive the same from us today.[67]

★

Some members have been quick to point out the shortcomings of the FBI, the CIA, and the FAA and claim more money will rectify the situation. I'm not so sure. Bureaucracies by nature are inefficient. The FBI and CIA records come up short. The FBI loses computers and guns and is careless with records. The CIA rarely provides timely intelligence.[68]

★ Civil Disobedience ★

Resistance need not be violent, but the civil disobedience that might be required involves confrontation with the state and invites possible imprisonment.[69]

Before the war in the Middle East spreads and becomes a world conflict, for which we'll be held responsible, or the liberties of all Americans become so suppressed we can no longer resist, much has to be done. Time is short but our course of action should be clear. Resistance to illegal and unconstitutional usurpation of our rights is required. **Each of us must choose which course of action we should take—education, conventional political action, or even peaceful civil disobedience, to bring about the necessary changes.**[70]

 Civil Liberties ★

Unfortunately, neither party has much concern for civil liberties.[71]

The real problem is that those who love the state too often advocate policies that lead to military action. At home they are quite willing to produce a crisis atmosphere and claim a war is needed to solve the problem. Under these conditions the people are more willing to bear the burden of paying for the war, and to carelessly sacrifice liberties, which they are told is necessary.[72]

We are continually being reminded that "9/11 has changed everything." **Unfortunately, the policy that needed most to be changed—that is our policy of foreign interventionism—has only been expanded.** There is no pretense any longer that a policy of humility in foreign affairs, without being the world's policeman and engaging in nation building, is worthy of consideration. We now live in a post-9/11 America where our government is going to make us safe no matter what it takes. We're expected to grin and bear it and adjust to every loss of our liberties in the name of patriotism and security.[73]

The war mentality, and the pervasive fear of an unidentified enemy, allows for a steady erosion of our liberties, and with

this our respect for self-reliance and confidence is lost. Just think of the self-sacrifice and the humiliation we go through at the airport screening process on a routine basis. Though there's no scientific evidence of any likelihood of liquids and gels being mixed on an airplane to make a bomb, billions of dollars are wasted throwing away toothpaste and hair spray and searching old women in wheelchairs.[74]

The erosion of our personal liberties started long before 9/11, but 9/11 accelerated the process. There are many things that motivate those who pursue this course—both well intentioned and malevolent. But it would not happen if the people remained vigilant, understood the importance of individual rights, and were unpersuaded that a need for security justifies the sacrifice of liberty—even if it's just now and then.[75]

Even though in every war in which we have been engaged, civil liberties have suffered, some have been restored after the war ended, but never completely. **This has resulted in a steady erosion of our liberties over the past 200 years.** Our government was originally designed to protect our liberties, but it has now instead become the usurper of those liberties.[76]

As our liberties here at home are diminished by the Patriot Act and national ID card legislation, we succumb to the temptation of all empires to neglect habeas corpus, employ torture tactics, and use secret imprisonment. These domestic and foreign policy trends reflect a morally bankrupt philosophy, devoid of any concern for liberty and the rule of law.[77]

★ Congress ★

It's been suggested we need to change course

and correct the way Congress is run. A good idea, but if we merely tinker with current attitudes about what role the federal government ought to play in our lives, it won't do much to solve the ethics crisis.[78]

Members of the United States Congress are often like crusaders in need of a cause. **When a cause is not readily available, or those that are do not meet well-established standards of political correctness, congressmen are willing to create one to suit their needs.**[79]

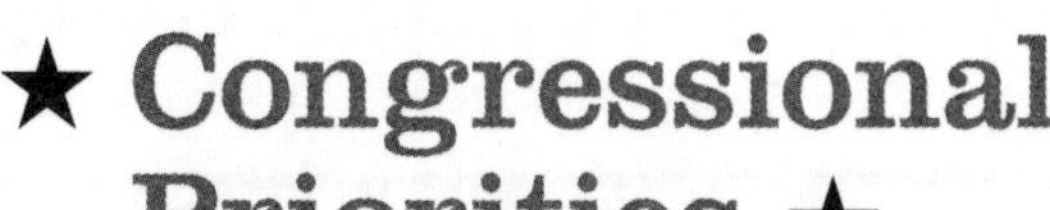

★ Congressional Priorities ★

Meanwhile, the Financial Services Committee, on which I sit, has begun the process of reauthorizing the Export-Import Bank, which uses taxpayer money to support business projects that cannot

attract capital in the market. Mr. Speaker, the Export-Import Bank's biggest beneficiaries are Boeing and communist China. I find it hard to believe that federal funding for Fortune 500 companies and China is a higher priority for most Americans than Medicaid and food stamps.[80]

We need to end the phony talk about "priorities" and recognize federal spending as the runaway freight train that it is. A federal government that spends $2.4 trillion in one year and consumes roughly one-third of the nation's GDP is far too large.[81]

I am also concerned that, by not applying the spending caps to international or military programs, this bill invites future Congresses to misplace priorities, and ignores a major source of fiscal imprudence.[82]

★ Conservatives ★

Conservatives in particular should be leery of anything that increases federal power, since centralized government power is traditionally the enemy of conservative values.[83]

The modern-day limited-government movement has been co-opted. The conservatives have failed in their effort to shrink the size of government. There has not been, nor will there soon be, a conservative revolution in Washington. Party control of the federal government has changed, but the inexorable growth in the size and scope of government has continued unabated. **The liberal arguments for limited government in personal affairs and foreign military adventurism were never seriously considered as part of this revolution.[84]**

One thing is certain: **Conservatives who worked and voted for less government in the Reagan years and welcomed the takeover of the U.S. Congress and the presidency in the 1990s and early 2000s were deceived.** Soon they will realize that the goal of limited government has been dashed and that their views no longer matter.[85]

★ Constitution ★

If you obey the Constitution though, you'll be a freer person than if you disobey it. If you allow the president to run wild and investigate and spy on people and start wars that aren't declared, you could lose your liberties.[86]

There's no logical reason to reject the restraints placed in the Constitution regarding our engaging in foreign conflicts unrelated to our national security. **The advice of the founders and our early presidents was sound then, and it's sound today.**[87]

Most of our mistakes can be laid at the doorstep of our failure to follow the Constitution.[88]

A policy that endorses peace over war, trade over sanctions, courtesy over arrogance, and liberty over coercion is in the tradition of the American Constitution and American idealism. It deserves consideration.[89]

★ Constitutional Liberties ★

The overriding goal should then be to rescue our constitutional liberties, which have been steadily eroded by those who claim that sacrificing civil liberties is required and legitimate in times of war—even the undeclared and vague war we're currently fighting.[90]

It's easy for elected officials in Washington to tell the American people that government will do whatever it takes to defeat terrorism. Such assurances inevitably are followed by proposals either to restrict the constitutional liberties of the American people or spend vast sums from the federal treasury.[91]

A strong separation of powers is at the heart of our Constitutional liberties.[92]

★ Counterfeiting ★

But if the Federal Reserve did not pick up the slack and create huge amounts of new credit and money out of thin air, interest rates would rise and call a halt to the charade. The people who suffer from a depreciated dollar don't understand why they suffer, while the people who benefit promote the corrupt system. The wealthy clean up on Wall Street, and the unsophisticated buy in as the market tops off. Wealth is transferred from one group to another, and it's all related to the system that allows politicians and the central banks to create money out of thin air. **It's literally legalized counterfeiting.**[93]

Counterfeiting money never creates wealth–it only steals wealth from the unsuspecting. The Federal Reserve creation of money is exactly the same. **Increasing the dollars in circulation can only diminish the value of each existing dollar.**[94]

★ Courts ★

Congress has the Constitutional authority to

rein in the federal courts' jurisdiction and the duty to preserve the states' republican forms of governments.[95]

Both the clear language of the United States Constitution and a long line of legal precedents make it clear that Congress has the authority to limit the Supreme Court's jurisdiction.[96]

The practice of judicial activism–legislating from the bench–is now standard procedure for many federal judges.[97]

They dismiss the doctrine of strict construction as outdated, instead treating the Constitution as fluid and malleable to create a desired outcome in any given case.[98]

For judges who see themselves as social activists, their vision of justice is more important than the letter of the law they are sworn to interpret and uphold.[99]

With the federal judiciary focused more on promoting a social agenda than on upholding the rule of law, Americans find themselves increasingly governed by judges they did not elect and cannot remove from office.[100]

The drafters of the Constitution gave Congress the power to limit federal jurisdiction to provide a check on out-of-control federal judges. **It is long past time we begin using our legitimate authority to protect the states and the people from judicial tyranny.**[101]

Allowing federal judges unfettered discretion to strike down state laws, or force a state to conform to the laws of another state, leads to centralization and loss of liberty.[102]

★ Debt ★

The system of special interest government that has evolved over the last several decades has given us a national debt of over eight trillion dollars, a debt that now expands by over 600 billion dollars each year. Our total obligations are estimated between fifteen and twenty trillion dollars. Most people realize the Social Security system, the Medicare system, and the new prescription drug plan are unfunded.[103]

It's important to note that total future obligations of the United States government are estimated at well over $70 trillion. These obligations obviously cannot be met. This indebtedness equates

to an average household share of the national debt of $474,000![104]

The term "national debt" really is a misnomer. It is not the nation's debt. Instead, it is the federal government's debt. **The American people did not spend the money, but they will have to pay it back.[105]**

The whole point of the debt ceiling law was to limit borrowing by forcing Congress into an open and presumably somewhat shameful vote when it wants to borrow more than a preset amount of money. Yet, since there have been no political consequences for members who vote to raise the debt limit and support the outrageous spending bills in the first place, **the debt limit has become merely another technicality on the road to bankruptcy.[106]**

★ Declaration of War ★

One of the greatest losses suffered these past sixty years from interventionism becoming an acceptable policy of both major parties is respect for the Constitution. Congress flatly has reneged on its huge responsibility to declare war. Going to war was never meant to be an executive decision, used indiscriminately with no resistance from Congress. The strongest attempt by Congress in the past sixty years to properly exert itself over foreign policy was the passage of the Foley Amendment, demanding no assistance be given to the Nicaraguan Contras. Even this explicit prohibition was flaunted by an earlier administration. [107]

When Congress accepts and assumes its awesome responsibility to declare war, as directed by the Constitution, fewer wars will be fought.[108]

The fact that Congress is not permitted under the Constitution to transfer the war power to a president was ignored. Only Congress can declare war, if we were inclined to follow the rule of law.[109]

Today, though, all the old reasons for going to war have been discredited, and are no longer used to justify continuing the war. Now we are told we must "complete the mission," and yet no one seems to know exactly what the mission is or when it can be achieved. By contrast, when war is properly declared against a country, we can expect an all-out effort until the country surrenders. Without a declaration of war as the Constitution requires, it's left to the president to decide when to start the war and when the war is over. We had sad experiences with this process in Korea and especially in Vietnam.[110]

You have to realize that the base of the Republican Party shrunk last year because of the war issue.

So that percentage represents less people. If you look at 65 to 70 percent of the American people, they want us out of there. They want the war over. In 2002, I offered an amendment to international relations to declare war, up or down, and it was, nobody voted for the war. And my argument was, if we want to go to war, and if we should go to war, the Congress should declare it. We don't go to war like we did in Vietnam and Korea because the wars never end.[111]

★

Deficit

Congress spends hundreds of billions of dollars in "emergency" supplemental bills to avoid the budgetary rules meant to hold down the deficit.[112]

No matter how hard the big spenders try to convince us otherwise, deficits do matter. But lowering the deficit through higher taxes won't solve anything.[113]

The amazing thing is that deficits and increases in the debt limit no longer have a stigma attached to them. Some demagoguery takes place, but the limit is easily raised.[114]

★ Democracy ★

Demanding an election in Palestinian Gaza resulted in enhancing the power of Hamas. The United States and Israel promptly rejected the results. So much for our support for democratically elected government.[115]

We claim to be spreading democracy in Iraq, but al Sadr has far more democratic support with the majority Shiites than our troops enjoy. **The problem is not a lack of democratic consensus; it is the antipathy toward our presence among most Iraqis.**[116]

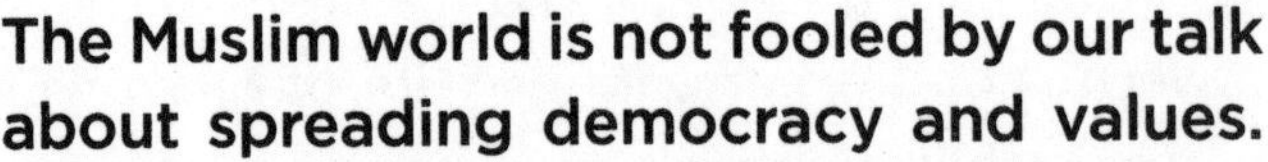

The Muslim world is not fooled by our talk about spreading democracy and values. The evidence is too overwhelming that we do not hesitate to support dictators and install puppet governments when it serves our interests. When democratic elections result in the elevation of a leader or party not to our liking, we do not hesitate for a minute to undermine that government. This hypocrisy is rarely recognized by the American people.[117]

Thankfully, our founding fathers understood the great dangers of a democracy. They insisted on a Constitutional republic with a weak central government and an executive branch beholden to the legislative branch in foreign affairs. The sooner we realize we can't afford this war, the better. We've gotten ourselves into a civil war within the Islamic community.[118]

Another amendment will create a chilling "Active Response Corps," to be made up of U.S. government bureaucrats and members of "non-governmental organizations." Its purpose will be to "stabilize" countries undergoing "democratic transition." This means that as soon as the National Endowment for Democracy-funded "people's revolutionaries" are able to seize power in the streets, U.S.-funded teams will be deployed to make sure they retain power. **All in the name of democracy, of course.**[119]

This bill continues to fund organizations such as the National Endowment for Democracy (NED), which as I have written before has very little to do with democracy. It is an organization that uses U.S. tax money to actually subvert democracy, by showering funding on favored political parties or movements overseas. It underwrites color-coded "people's revolutions" overseas that look more like pages out of Lenin's writings on stealing power than genuine indigenous democratic movements. The NED used American taxpayer dollars to attempt to guarantee that certain candidates overseas are winners and others are losers in the electoral processes overseas. What kind of message do we think this sends to foreign states? **The National Endowment for Democracy should receive no funding at all, but this bill continues to funnel tens of millions of dollars to that unaccountable organization.**[120]

One major contributing factor for the past hundred years is our serious misunderstanding of the dangers of pure democracy. The founders detested democracy and avoided the use of the word in all the early documents. Today, most Americans accept without question a policy of sacrificing life, property, and dollars to force "democracy" on a country 6,000 miles away. This tells us how little opposition there is to "democracy." **No one questions the principle that a majority electorate should be allowed to rule the country, dictate rights, and redistribute wealth.**[121]

★ Depreciation of the Dollar ★

Economic strength and military power contribute to the trust in a currency; in today's world trust in the U.S. dollar is not earned and therefore fragile. The history of the dollar, being as good as gold up until 1971, is helpful in maintaining an artificially higher value for the dollar than deserved.[122]

★

Foreign policy contributes to the crisis when the spending to maintain our worldwide military commitments becomes prohibitive and inflationary pressures accelerate. But the real crisis hits when the world realizes the king has no clothes, in that the dollar has no backing, and we face a military setback even greater than we already are experiencing in Iraq. Our token friends may quickly transform into vocal enemies once the attack on the dollar begins.[123]

Small businesses and individual enterprises suffer more than the financial elite, who borrow large sums before the money loses value.[124]

The current surge in gold prices—which reflects our dollar's devaluation—is warning us to pay closer attention to our fiscal, monetary, entitlement, and foreign policy.[125]

A hundred years ago it was called "dollar diplomacy." After World War II, and especially after the fall of the Soviet Union in 1989, that policy evolved into "dollar hegemony." But after all these many years of great success, our dollar dominance is coming to an end.[126]

The prime beneficiaries of a paper money system are those who use the money early—governments, politicians, bankers, international corporations, and the military-industrial complex. Those who suffer most are the ones at the end of the money chain—the people forced to use depreciated dollars to buy urgently needed goods and services to survive. And guess what? **By then their money is worth less, prices soar, and their standard of living goes down.**[127]

Once Rome converted from a republic to an empire, she depreciated her currency to pay the bills. This eventually led to Rome's downfall. That is exactly what America is facing unless we change our ways. Now this is a real scandal worth worrying about.[128]

★ Diplomacy ★

Containment and diplomacy are far superior to confronting a potential enemy, and are less costly and far less dangerous—especially when there's no evidence that our national security is being threatened.[129]

Diplomacy and trade can accomplish goals that military intervention cannot—and they certainly are less costly.[130]

A policy of trade and peace, and a willingness to use diplomacy, is far superior to the foreign policy that has evolved over the past sixty years.[131]

★ Draft ★

Some members of Congress, intent on equitably distributing the suffering among all Americans, want to bring back the draft. Administration officials vehemently deny making any concrete plans for a draft. **But why should we believe this?** Look what happened when so many believed the reasons given for our preemptive invasion of Iraq.[132]

Selective Service officials admit running a check of their lists of available young men. If the draft is reinstated, we probably will include young women as well to serve the god of "equality." Conscription is slavery, plain and simple.[133]

The Department of Defense, in response to calls to reinstate the draft, has confirmed that **conscription serves no military need.** Defense officials from both parties have repudiated it.[134]

Some say the eighteen-year-old draftee "owes it" to his (or her, since HR 163 makes women eligible for the draft) country. Hogwash! It just as easily could be argued that a fifty-year-old chicken hawk, who promotes war and places innocent young people in danger, owes more to the country than the eighteen-year-old being denied his (or her) liberty.[135]

All drafts are unfair. All eighteen- and nineteen-year-olds are never drafted. By its very nature a draft must be discriminatory. **All drafts hit the most vulnerable young people, as the elites learn quickly how to avoid the risks of combat.**[136]

The draft encourages wars with neither purpose nor moral justification, wars that too often are not even declared by the Congress.[137]

A free society must always resort to volunteers. **Tyrants think nothing of forcing men to fight and serve in wrongheaded wars.**[138]

A true fight for survival and defense of America would elicit, I am sure, the assistance of every able-bodied man and woman. This is not the case with wars of mischief far away from home, which we have experienced often in the past century.[139]

A return to the spirit of the republic would mean that a draft would never be used and all able-bodied persons would be willing to volunteer in defense of their liberty.[140]

★ Economics ★

The economic impossibility of this system guarantees that the harder government tries to satisfy the unlimited demands, the worse the problems become. **We won't be able to pay the bills forever, and eventually our ability to borrow and print new money must end.** This dependency on government will guarantee anger when the money runs out.[141]

Economic law eventually will prevail. Runaway military and entitlement spending cannot be sustained. We can tax the private economy only so much, and borrowing from foreigners is

limited by the total foreign debt and our current account deficit. It will be difficult to continue this spending spree without significantly higher interest rates and further devaluation of the dollar. [142]

Economic realities will prevail, regardless of the enthusiasm by most members of Congress for a continued expansion of the welfare state and support for our dangerously aggressive foreign policy. **The welfare/warfare state will come to an end when the dollar fails and the money simply runs out.**[143]

A strong case can be made that our economy is not nearly as robust as our government statistics claim.[144]

★ Education ★

Of the twenty congressionally authorized functions granted by the Constitution, education is

not one of them. That should be enough of a reason not to be involved, but there's no evidence of any benefit, and statistics show that great harm has resulted. It has cost us hundreds of billions of dollars, yet we continue the inexorable march toward total domination of our educational system by Washington bureaucrats and politicians. It makes no sense![145]

The best thing we could do now is pass a bill to give parents a $3,000 tax credit for each child they educate. This would encourage competition and allow a lot more choice for parents struggling to help their children get a decent education.[146]

The people of the 14th District—and people from around the nation—are sick of programs like the president's "Goals 2000," which are more about social and political correctness than education; they are tired of seeing classrooms turned into vehicles for social engineering, instead of as places for reading and math.[147]

Instead of fostering open dialogue and wide-ranging intellectual inquiry, the main effect of the "Academic Bill of Rights" will be to further stifle debate about controversial topics. This is because many administrators will order their professors not to discuss contentious and divisive subjects, in order to avoid a possible confrontation with the federal government.[148]

★ Empathy ★

The toughest task is analyzing what we do from their perspective. **We should try harder to place ourselves in the shoes of those who live in the Arab countries where our efforts currently are concentrated.** We are outraged by a Muslim country that would even consider the death penalty for a Christian convert. But many Muslims see all that we do as a reflection of Western Christianity, which to them includes Europe and America. They see everything in terms of religion. When our bombs and sanctions kill hundreds of thousands of their citizens, they see it as an attack on their religion by Christians. To them our actions represent a crusade to change their culture and their political systems. They do not see us as having noble intentions. Cynicism and realism tell them we're involved in the Middle East to secure the oil we need.[149]

What if England had had a law like this in place in 1993 during the Waco debacle? How would we as Americans have reacted when the British government banned all our goods from being sold in the United Kingdom because of the actions of our federal government against a religious minority? We would have been outraged. Can we expect less from anyone else? **I think we should be very careful about casting stones.**[150]

★

The question we must ask ourselves is how would we react if we had Chinese airplanes flying up and down our coast and occupying the airspace of the Gulf of Mexico?[151]

★

★ Empire ★

Empires always fail, and expenses always exceed projections. Harmful unintended consequences are the rule, not the exception. Welfare for the poor is inefficient and wasteful. The beneficiaries are rarely the poor themselves, but instead the politicians, bureaucrats, or the wealthy. **The same is true of all foreign aid—it's nothing more than a program that steals from the poor in a rich country and gives to the rich leaders of a poor country.[152]**

★

Our whole economic system depends on continuing the current monetary arrangement, which means recycling the dollar is crucial. Currently, we borrow over $700 billion every year from our gracious benefactors, who work hard and take our paper for their goods. Then we borrow all the money we need to secure the empire (Department of Defense budget $450 billion) plus more.[153]

★ Enhancing the State ★

A more sophisticated and less well-known technique for enhancing the state is the manipulation and transfer of wealth through the fiat monetary system operated by the secretive Federal Reserve. Protestors against this unconstitutional system of paper money are considered unpatriotic criminals and at times are imprisoned for their beliefs. The fact that, according to the Constitution, only

gold and silver are legal tender and paper money is outlawed, matters little. The principle of patriotism is turned on its head.[154]

Because the crisis atmosphere of war supports the growth of the state, any problem invites an answer by declaring "war"—even on social and economic issues. This elicits patriotism in support of various government solutions while enhancing the power of the state.[155]

★

★ Entangling Alliances ★

Entangling alliances with no one means no foreign aid to Pakistan, or Egypt, or Israel, or anyone else for that matter. If an American citizen determines a foreign country or cause is worthy of their money, let them send it, and encourage their neighbors to send money too, but **our government has no authority**

to use hard-earned American taxpayer dollars to mire us in these nightmarishly complicated, no-win entangling alliances.[156]

★

★ Exaggerated Enemy ★

Nobody wins elections by promising to take us to war. But once elected, many politicians greatly exaggerate the threat posed by a potential enemy—and the people too often carelessly accept the dubious reasons given to justify wars. Opposition arises only when the true costs are felt here at home.[157]

★

★ Executive Orders ★

Since 9/11, presidential signing statements designating portions of legislation that the president does

not intend to follow, though not legal under the Constitution, have enormously multiplied. Unconstitutional executive orders are numerous and mischievous and need to be curtailed.[158]

Some of the least noticed and least discussed changes in the law were the changes made to the Insurrection Act of 1807 and to Posse Comitatus by the Defense Authorization Act of 2007. **These changes pose a threat to the survival of our republic by giving the president the power to declare martial law for as little reason as to restore "public order."** The 1807 act severely restricted the president in his use of the military within the United States borders, and the Posse Comitatus Act of 1878 strengthened these restrictions with strict oversight by Congress. The new law allows the president to circumvent the restrictions of both laws. The Insurrection Act has now become the "Enforcement of the Laws to Restore Public Order Act". This is hardly a title that suggests that the authors cared about or understood the nature of a Constitutional republic.[159]

With the "power" of the executive order, presidents can commit our troops to undeclared wars, destroy industries or make unprecedented social-policy changes. And they remain unaccountable because **often these actions occur behind the door of the Oval Office, are distributed without notice, and then executed in stealth.**[160]

While there is a role for executive orders so that the president may execute his authorities and direct his employees, for far too many years, the illegitimate uses have overshadowed the legitimate. Presidents have issued executive orders that take on the force of law.[161]

Because of the FDA's [Food and Drug Administration] censorship of truthful health claims, millions of Americans may suffer with diseases and other health care problems they may have avoided by using dietary supplements. For example, the FDA prohibited consumers from learning how folic acid reduces the risk of neural tube defects for four years after the Centers for Disease Control and Prevention recommended every woman of childbearing age take folic acid supplements to reduce neural tube defects. This FDA action contributed to an estimated 10,000 cases of preventable neutral tube defects![162]

The FDA also continues to prohibit consumers from learning about the scientific evidence that glucosamine and chondroitin sulfate are effective in the treatment of osteoarthritis; that omega-3 fatty acids may reduce the risk of sudden death heart attack; and that calcium may reduce the risk of bone fractures. [163]

The Health Freedom Protection Act will force the FDA to at last comply with the commands of Congress, the First Amendment, and the American people by codifying the First Amendment standards adopted by the federal courts.[164]

The American people have made it clear they do not want the federal government to interfere with their access to dietary supplements, yet the FDA and the Federal Trade Commission continue to engage in heavy-handed attempts to restrict such access.[165]

★ Fear ★

Fear is generated to garner popular support for the proposed government action, even when some liberty has to be sacri-

ficed. This leads to a society that is systemically driven toward fear—fear that gives the monstrous government more and more authority and control over our lives and property.[166]

Fear is constantly generated by politicians to rally the support of the people.[167]

In all instances where fear is generated and used to expand government control, it's safe to say the problems behind the fears were not caused by the free-market economy, or too much privacy, or excessive liberty.[168]

It's easy to generate fear, fear that too often becomes excessive, unrealistic, and difficult to curb. This is important: **It leads to even more demands for government action than the perpetrators of the fear actually anticipated.**[169]

Generating exaggerated fear to justify and promote attacks on private property is commonplace. It serves to inflame resentment between the producers in society and the so-called victims, whose demands grow exponentially.[170]

It is, however, in foreign affairs that governments have most abused fear to generate support for an agenda that under normal circumstances would have been rejected. **For decades our administrations have targeted one supposed "Hitler" after another to gain support for military action against a particular country.** Today we have three choices termed the axis of evil: Iran, Iraq, or North Korea.[171]

The world is much too dangerous, we're told, and therefore we must be prepared to fight at a moment's notice, regardless of the cost. **If the public could not be manipulated by politicians' efforts to instill needless fear, fewer wars would be fought and far fewer lives would be lost.**[172]

Mr. Speaker, anyone needing proof that federal funding leads to federal control should examine HR 609, the "College Access and Opportunity Act." HR 609 imposes several new federal mandates on colleges, and extends numerous existing mandates. HR 609 proves the prophetic soundness of warnings that federal higher education programs would lead to federal control of higher education.[173]

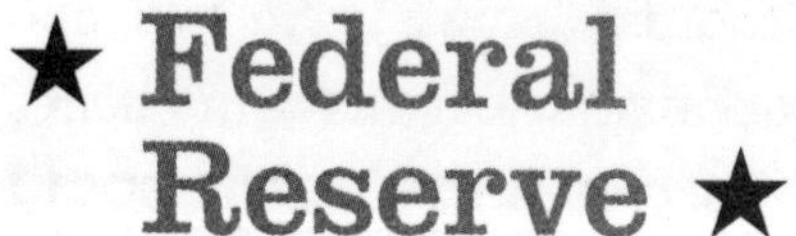

★ Federal Reserve ★

When deficits are excessive, as they are today, the Fed creates new dollars out of thin air to buy Treasury bills and keep interest rates artificially low. But when new money is created out of nothing, the money already in circulation loses value. Once this is recognized, prices rise—some more rapidly than others. That's what we see today with the cost of energy.[174]

Exploding deficits, due to runaway entitlement spending and the cost of dangerous militarism, create pressure for the Fed to inflate the money supply. This contributes greatly to the higher prices we all claim to oppose.[175]

The number of dollars created by the Federal Reserve, and through the fractional reserve bank-

ing system, is crucial in determining how the market assesses the relationship of the dollar and gold. Though there's a strong correlation, it's not instantaneous or perfectly predictable. There are many variables to consider, but in the long term the dollar price of gold represents past inflation of the money supply. Equally important, it represents the anticipation of how much new money will be created in the future. This introduces the factor of trust and confidence in our monetary authorities and our politicians. **And these days the American people are casting a vote of "no confidence" in this regard, and for good reasons.**[176]

There's no single measurement that reveals what the Fed has done in the recent past or tells us exactly what it's about to do in the future.[177]

Forget about the lip service given to transparency by new Fed Chairman Bernanke. Not only

is this administration one of the most secretive across the board in our history, the current Fed firmly supports denying the most important measurement of current monetary policy to Congress, the financial community, and the American public. Because of a lack of interest and poor understanding of monetary policy, Congress has expressed essentially no concern about the significant change in reporting statistics on the money supply.[178]

Beginning in March, though planned before Bernanke arrived at the Fed, the central bank discontinued compiling and reporting the monetary aggregate known as M3. M3 is the best description of how quickly the Fed is creating new money and credit. Common sense tells us that a government central bank creating new money out of thin air depreciates the value of each dollar in circulation. Yet this report is no longer available to us and Congress makes no demands to receive it. Though M3 is the most helpful statistic to

track Fed activity, it by no means tells us everything we need to know about trends in monetary policy.[179]

Congress created the Federal Reserve, yet it had no Constitutional authority to do so.[180]

We need more transparency in how the Federal Reserve carries out monetary policy, and we need it soon.[181]

Congress created the Federal Reserve System in 1913. Between then and 1971 the principle of sound money was systematically undermined. **Between 1913 and 1971, the Federal Reserve found it much easier to expand the money supply at will for financing war or manipulating the economy with little resistance from Congress**—while benefiting the special interests that influence government.[182]

★

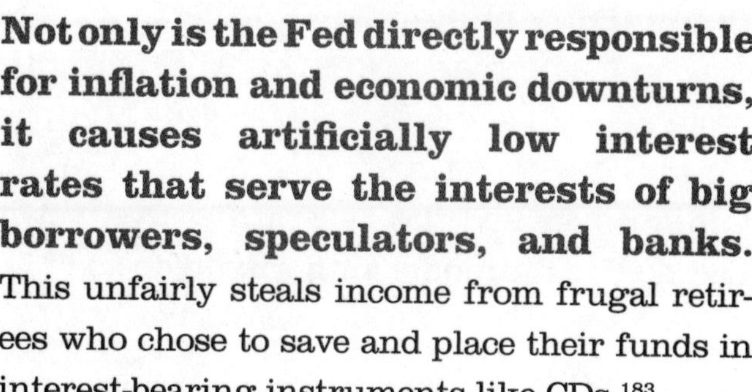

Not only is the Fed directly responsible for inflation and economic downturns, it causes artificially low interest rates that serve the interests of big borrowers, speculators, and banks. This unfairly steals income from frugal retirees who chose to save and place their funds in interest-bearing instruments like CDs.[183]

★

The Fed's great power over the money supply, interest rates, the business cycle, unemployment, and inflation is wielded with essentially no Congressional oversight or understanding.[184]

★

★ Federalization ★

Opponents of increased federalization of higher education should be especially concerned about HR 609's "Academic Bill of Rights." This provision takes a step toward complete federal control of college curricula, grading, and teaching practices. While the provision is worded as a "sense of Congress," **the clear intent is to intimidate college administrators into ensuring professors' lectures and lesson plans meet with federal approval.**[185]

★ Fiat Money ★

Though great economic harm comes from a government monopoly fiat monetary system, the loss of liberty associated with it is equally troubling.[186]

The founders understood this great danger, and voted overwhelmingly to reject "emitting bills of credit," the term they used for paper or fiat money. It's too bad the knowledge and advice of our founders, and their mandate in the Constitution, are ignored today at our great peril.[187]

Paper money permits the regressive inflation tax to be passed off on the poor and the middle class.[188]

Without a fiat monetary system wars would be very difficult to finance, since the people would never tolerate the taxes required to pay for it.[189]

In the short run, the issuer of a fiat reserve currency can accrue great economic benefits. In the long run, it poses a threat to the country issuing the world currency. In this case that's the United States. As long as foreign countries take our dollars in return for real goods, we come out ahead. This is a benefit many in Congress fail to recognize, as they bash China for maintaining a positive trade balance with us. But this leads to a loss of manufacturing jobs to overseas markets, as we become more dependent on others and less self-sufficient.[190]

The consequences of this system, fully in place for the past thirty-four years, are astronomical and impossible to accurately measure. Industries go offshore, and the jobs follow. Price inflation eats away at the middle class, and deficits soar while spending escalates rapidly as Congress hopes to keep up with the problems it created.[191]

Simply put, printing money to pay for federal spending dilutes the value of the dollar, which causes higher prices for goods and services.[192]

The fact that the U.S. dollar is the principal reserve currency of the world gives us a benefit that others do not enjoy. It allows us to export paper dollars and import goods manufactured in countries with cheap labor. It also allows us to finance the welfare/warfare state with cheap loans from China and Japan. **It's a good deal for us but according to economic law must come to an end, and the end will be messy for the U.S. consumer and for world trade.**[193]

★

★ Financial Crisis ★

We face a coming financial crisis. Our current account deficit is more than $600 billion annually. Our foreign debt is more than $3 trillion. Foreigners now own over $1.4 trillion of our Treasury and mortgage debt. We must borrow $3 billion from foreigners every business day to maintain our extravagant spending. **Our national debt now is increasing $600 billion per year, and guess what, we print over $600 billion per year to keep the charade going. But there is a limit, and I'm fearful we're fast approaching it.**[194]

★ Fiscal Responsibility ★

Instead of the smoke-and-mirrors approach of HR 4241, Congress should begin the journey toward fiscal responsibility by declaring a 10 percent reduction in real spending, followed by a renewed commitment to reduce spending in a manner consistent with our obligation to uphold the Constitution and the priorities of the American people. This is the only way to make real progress on reducing spending without cutting programs for the poor while increasing funding for programs that benefit foreign governments and corporate interests.[195]

To hear big spending, pro-tax politicians claim they represent fiscal responsibility strains the limits of believability.[196]

★ Foreign Aid ★

We either subsidize people or we bomb them. Why not try another option? [197]

I believe that the Millennium Challenge Account (MCA) may be one of the worst foreign policy blunders yet—and among the most costly. It is advertised as a whole new kind of foreign aid—apparently an honest admission that the old system of foreign aid does not work. But rather than get rid of the old, bad system of foreign aid in favor of this "new and improved" system, we are keeping both systems and thereby doubling our foreign aid. I guess it is easy to be generous with other people's money. [198]

Sending U.S. aid money into countries that are pursuing sound economic policies will not help these economies. On the contrary, **an external infusion of money to governments meet-**

ing the economic criteria will actually obscure areas where an economy is inefficient and unproductive.[199]

The wisest approach to international economic development is for the United States to lead by example, to reembrace the kind of economic policies that led us to become wealthy in the first place. **This means less government, less taxation, no foreign meddling.**[200]

Demonstrating the effectiveness of limited government in creating wealth would be the greatest gift we could send overseas.[201]

★ Foreign Policy ★

If you keep living in this dream land of saying that they attack us because we're free and prosperous, believe me, we're never going to get a sensible foreign policy.[202]

The major obstacle to a sensible foreign policy is the fiction about what patriotism means. Today patriotism has come to mean blind support for the government and its policies. In earlier times patriotism meant having the willingness and courage to challenge government policies regardless of popular perceptions.[203]

Our support for dictatorial Arab leaders is a thorn in the side of the large Muslim population in the Middle East, and one of the main reasons Osama bin Laden declared war against us. We talk of democracy and self-determination, but the masses of people in the Middle East see through our hypocrisy when we support the Sunni secular dictators in Saudi Arabia, Egypt, and Jordan, and at one time, Saddam Hussein.[204]

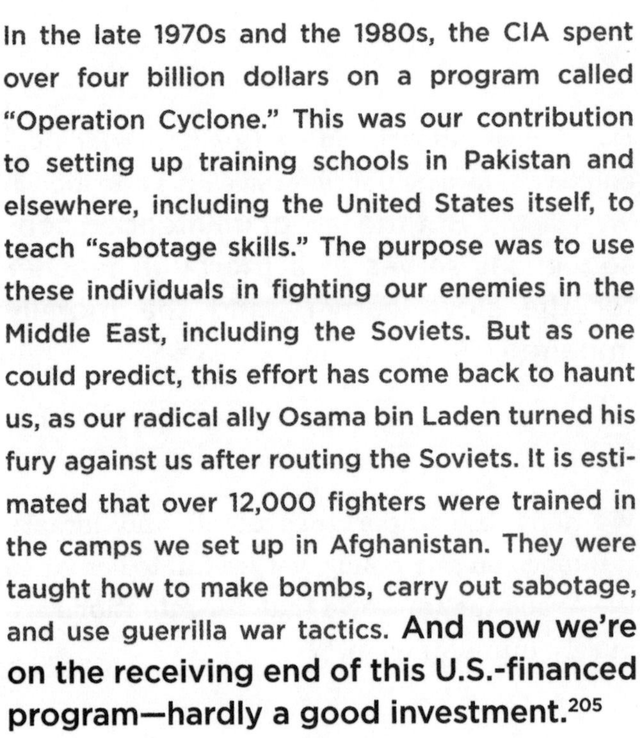
In the late 1970s and the 1980s, the CIA spent over four billion dollars on a program called "Operation Cyclone." This was our contribution to setting up training schools in Pakistan and elsewhere, including the United States itself, to teach "sabotage skills." The purpose was to use these individuals in fighting our enemies in the Middle East, including the Soviets. But as one could predict, this effort has come back to haunt us, as our radical ally Osama bin Laden turned his fury against us after routing the Soviets. It is estimated that over 12,000 fighters were trained in the camps we set up in Afghanistan. They were taught how to make bombs, carry out sabotage, and use guerrilla war tactics. **And now we're on the receiving end of this U.S.-financed program—hardly a good investment.**[205]

Unfortunately, regime change, nation building, policing the world, and protecting "our oil" still constitute an acceptable policy by the leaders of both major parties.[206]

Moral, constitutional, and legal arguments for a less aggressive foreign policy receive little attention in Washington. **But the law of unintended consequences serves as a thorough teacher for the slow learners and the morally impaired.**[207]

We deny the importance of oil and Israel's influence on our policy, yet we fail to convince the Arab/Muslim world that our intentions are purely humanitarian.[208]

The mess we face in the Middle East and Afghanistan, and the threat of terrorism within our own borders, is not a result of the policies of this administration alone. Problems have

been building for many years and have only gotten much worse with our most recent policy of forcibly imposing regime change in Iraq. We must recognize that the stalemate in Korea, the loss in Vietnam, and the quagmire in Iraq and Afghanistan all result from the same flawed foreign policy of interventionism that our government has pursued for over one hundred years. It would be overly simplistic to say the current administration alone is responsible for the mess in Iraq.[209]

Changing our policy of meddling in the affairs of others won't come quickly or easily. But a few signals to indicate a change in our attitude would go a long way to bringing peace to a troubled land. We must soon, and Congress can do this through the budget process, stop the construction of all permanent bases in Iraq and any other Muslim country in the region. **Think of how we would react if the Chinese had the military edge on us and laid claims to the Gulf of Mexico, building bases within the**

United States in order to promote their superior way of life.[210]

The time will come when our policies dealing with foreign affairs will change for the better. But that will be because we can no longer afford the extravagance of war.[211]

Congress should make America safer by expanding liberty and refocusing our foreign policy on defending this nation's vital interests, rather than expanding the welfare state and wasting American blood and treasure on quixotic crusades to "democratize" the world.[212]

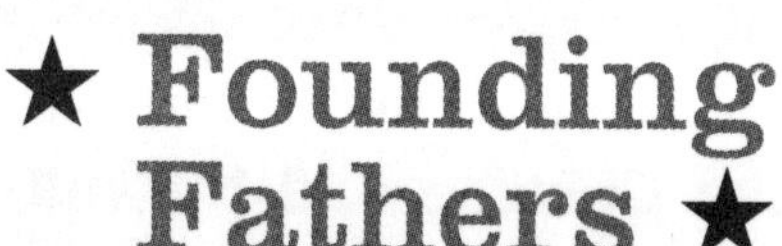

★ Founding Fathers ★

When we look at global situations today, the

words of our founding fathers are becoming more relevant daily.[213]

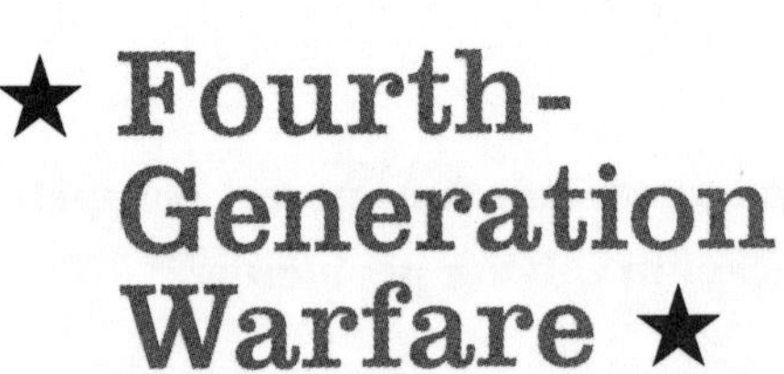

★ Fourth-Generation Warfare ★

Our inability to adapt to the tactics of fourth-generation warfare compounds our military failure. Unless we understand this, even doubling our troop strength will not solve the problems created by our occupation.[214]

★ Free Market ★

When the free market is allowed to work, it's the consumer who ultimately determines price and quality, with labor and business accommodating consumer choices. **Once this process is distorted by government, prices**

rise excessively, labor costs and profits are negatively affected, and problems emerge.[215]

Bureaucratic management can never compete with the free market in solving problems.[216]

I happen to think that the market can deliver any service better than the government can.[217]

Until the Congress realizes that the economy cannot be managed by a group of economists, no matter how large or how brilliant the group may be, the result will be the same. Inflation will continue to rise, and the American people will continue to grow poorer.[218]

There should be no distinction between commercial speech and political speech.[219]

Speech is speech, regardless of the setting. There is no legal distinction between religious expression and political expression; both are equally protected by the First Amendment. **Religious believers do not drop their political opinions at the door of their place of worship, nor do they disregard their faith at the ballot box.[220]**

★

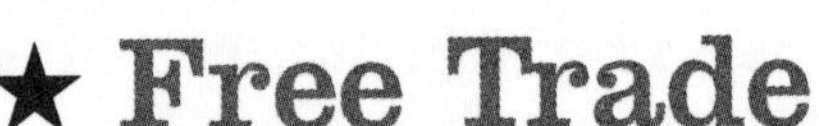

Both parties are split over trade, with mixed debates between outright protectionists and those who endorse government-managed trade agreements that masquerade as "free trade." **It's virtually**

impossible to find anyone who supports hands-off free trade, defended by the moral right of all citizens to spend their money as they see fit, without being subject to any special interest.[221]

Free trade is beneficial because it is a moral right.[222]

Free trade does not require management. It is implied here on conversation on the House floor so often that free trade is equivalent to say we will turn over the management of trade to the World Trade Organization, which serves special interests. **Well, that is not free trade; that is a misunderstanding of free trade.**[223]

Free trade is the ability of an individual or a corporation to buy goods and spend their money as they

see fit, and this provides tremendous economic benefits.[224]

★

★ Freedom ★

Freedom brings people together.[225]

★

This is my freedom message. People have to be left alone.[226]

★

We're losing our prosperity because we're losing our freedom.[227]

★

Freedom is not defined by safety. Freedom is defined by the ability of citizens to live without government interference. Government cannot create a world without risks, nor would we really wish to live in such a fictional place. Only a totalitarian society would even claim absolute safety as a worthy ideal, because it would require total state control over its citizens' lives. **Liberty has meaning only if we still believe in it when terrible things happen and a false government security blanket beckons.**[228]

★ Fund-Raising ★

They said if the candidate doesn't call and pander to special interests, he or she can't raise enough money. But here, we found out the campaign is very spontaneous and volunteers are coming.[229]

★ Future ★

Yes, Mr. Speaker, there is a lot of anger in this country. Much of it is justified; some of it is totally unnecessary and misdirected. The only thing that can lessen this anger is an informed

public, a better understanding of economic principles, a rejection of foreign intervention, and a strict adherence to the Constitutional rule of law. This will be difficult to achieve, but it's not impossible and well worth the effort.[230]

★ Gas Prices ★

An attack on Iran, coupled with our continued presence in Iraq, could hike gas prices to $5 or $6 per gallon here at home. **By contrast, a sensible approach toward Iran could quickly lower oil prices by $20 per barrel.[231]**

If we want to do something about gas prices, we should demand and vote for greatly reduced welfare and military spending, a balanced budget, and fewer regulations that interfere with the market development of alternative fuels.[232]

All subsidies and special benefits to energy companies should be ended. And in the meantime let's eliminate federal gas taxes at the pump.[233]

Interestingly, the cost of oil and gas is actually much higher than we pay at the retail level. Much of the Department of Defense budget is spent protecting "our" oil supplies, and if such spending is factored in gasoline probably costs us more than $5 a gallon. The sad irony is that this military effort to secure cheap oil supplies inevitably backfires, and actually curtails supplies and boosts prices at the pump.[234]

Last summer the market worked efficiently after Katrina—gas hit $3 a gallon, but soon supplies increased, usage went down, and the price returned to $2.[235]

★ Gold ★

Much can be learned by understanding what the rising dollar price of gold means.[236]

Holding gold is protection or insurance against government's proclivity to debase its currency. The purchasing power of gold goes up not because it's a so-called good investment; it goes up in value only because the paper currency goes down in value. In our current situation, that means the dollar.[237]

The point is that most who buy gold do so to protect against a depreciating currency rather than as an investment in the classical sense. Americans understand this less than citizens of other countries; some nations have suffered from severe monetary inflation that literally led to the destruction of their national currency.[238]

A soaring gold price is a vote of "no confidence" in the central bank and the dollar. This certainly was the case in 1979 and 1980. Today, gold prices reflect a growing restlessness with the increasing money supply, our budgetary and trade deficits, our unfunded liabilities, and the inability of Congress and the administration to rein in runaway spending.[239]

The value of gold is remarkably stable.[240]

The dollar price of gold reflects dollar depreciation.[241]

Since gold has proven to be the real money of the ages, we see once again a shift in

wealth from the West to the East, just as we saw a loss of our industrial base in the same direction. Though Treasury officials deny any U.S. sales or loans of our official gold holdings, no audits are permitted, so no one can be certain.[242]

The special nature of the dollar as the reserve currency of the world has allowed this game to last longer than it would have otherwise. But the fact that gold has gone from $252 to over $600 per ounce means there is concern about the future of the dollar. The higher the price for gold, the greater the concern for the dollar. Instead of dwelling on the dollar price of gold, we should be talking about the depreciation of the dollar. In 1934 a dollar was worth 1/20th of an ounce of gold; $20 bought an ounce of gold. Today a dollar is worth 1/600th of an ounce of gold, meaning it takes $600 to buy one ounce of gold.[243]

★ Gold Standard ★

Counterfeiting the nation's money is a serious offense. The founders were especially adamant about avoiding the chaos, inflation, and destruction associated with the Continental dollar. **That's why the Constitution is clear that only gold and silver should be legal tender in the United States.**[244]

Historically, paper money never has lasted for long periods of time, while gold has survived thousands of years of attacks by political interests and big government.[245]

Certainly geopolitical events in the Middle East under a gold standard would not alter its price, though they could affect the supply of oil and cause oil prices to rise.[246]

The harmful effects of the business cycle are virtually eliminated with an honest gold standard.[247]

Saving and thrift are encouraged by a gold standard; and discouraged by paper money.[248]

A sharply rising gold price is a vote of "no confidence" in Congress' ability to control the budget, the Fed's ability to control the money supply, and the administration's ability to bring stability to the Middle East.[249]

Ultimately, the gold price is a measurement of trust in the currency and the politicians who run the country. It's been that way for a long time, and is not about to change.[250]

Economic law dictates reform at some point. But should we wait until the dollar is 1/1000 of an ounce of gold or 1/2000 of an ounce of gold? **The longer we wait, the more people suffer, and the more difficult reforms become.**[251]

The amount of gold is unimportant; the main thing is that you honor what you have. If you don't seem to have enough gold, the prices just go down and accommodate. So that usually is not a problem, because gold hangs around and increases automatically about 3 percent per year.[252]

Since the last link to gold was severed in 1971, the dollar has lost 92 percent of its value relative to gold, with gold going from $35 to $450 per ounce.[253]

It has been said, rightly, that he who holds the gold makes the rules.[254]

★ Government ★

When you fill up your car, and it's $3 a gallon, or $4 or $5 a gallon, don't blame price gouging. Blame the government for a bad monetary policy and a bad foreign policy.[255]

Generally speaking, there are two controlling forces that determine the nature of government: the people's concern for their economic self-interests and the philosophy of those who hold positions of power and influence in any particular government. Under Soviet communism the workers believed their economic best interests were being served while a few dedicated theoreticians placed themselves in positions of power. Likewise, the intellectual leaders of the American Revolution were few but rallied the colonists to risk all to overthrow a tyrannical king.[256]

Since the use of power to achieve political ends is accepted, pervasive, and ever expanding, popular support for various programs is achieved by creating fear. Sometimes the fear is concocted out of thin air, but usually it's created by wildly exaggerating a problem or incident that does not warrant the proposed government "solution." Often government caused the problem in the first place. The irony, of course, is that government action rarely solves any problem but rather worsens existing problems or creates altogether new ones.[257]

The fact is a majority of American citizens expect the federal government to provide for every need, without considering whether government causes many economic problems in the first place.[258]

If solutions to America's problems won't be found in the frequent clamor for more government, it's still up to Congress to explain how our problems develop–and how solutions can be found in an atmosphere of liberty, private property, and a free market order.[259]

The big government nanny-state is based on the assumption that free markets can't provide the maximum good for the largest number of people. It assumes people are not smart or responsible enough to take care of themselves, and thus their needs must be filled through the government's forcible redistribution of wealth.[260]

Everyone is aware of the law of unintended consequences. Most members of Congress understand that government actions can have unintended consequences, yet few quit voting for government "solutions"—always hoping there won't be any particular unintended consequences this time. **They keep hoping there will be less harmful complications from the "solution" that they currently support.**[261]

Government has too much control over people and the market, making the temptation and incentive to influence government irresistible and to a degree necessary.[262]

Governments should just get out of the way and let individuals make their own decisions about how they want to relate to the world.[263]

It's time we reconsider the real purpose of government in a society that professes to be free—**protection of liberty, peaceful commerce, and keeping itself out of our lives, our economy, our pocketbooks, and certainly out of the affairs of foreign nations.**[264]

Voting on bills before members read them makes a mockery of representative government and cheats voters who sent us here to make informed decisions on public policy. [265]

This system of government is coming to an end—a fact that significantly contributes to the growing anxiety of most Americans, especially those who pay the bills and receive little in return from the corrupt system that has evolved over the decades.[266]

The theft that the federal government commits against its citizens, and the power that Congress has assumed illegally, are the real crimes that need to be dealt with.[267]

Even under today's flawed system of democratic government, which is dedicated to redistributing property by force, a lot could be accomplished if government attracted men and women of goodwill and character. Members could refuse to yield to the temptations of office and reject the path to a lobbying career. But it seems once government adopts the rules of immorality, some of the participants in the process yield to the temptation as well, succumbing to the belief that the new moral standards are acceptable. [268]

A free nation, as it moves toward authoritarianism, tolerates and hides a lot of abuse in the system.[269]

Whether government programs are promoted for "good" causes (helping the poor), or bad causes (permitting a military-industrial complex to capitalize on war profits), the principles of the market are undermined. Eventually nearly everyone becomes dependent on the system of deficits, borrowing, printing press money, and the special interest budget process that distributes loot by majority vote.[270]

Today most business interests and the poor are dependent on government handouts. Education and medical care [are] almost completely controlled and regulated by an overpowering central government. We have come to accept our role as world policemen and nation builder with little question, despite the bad results and an inability to pay the bills. The question is, what will it take to bring about the changes in policy needed to reverse this dangerous trend? The answer is: quite a lot. And unfortunately it's not on the horizon. It probably won't come until there is a rejection of the dollar as the safest and strongest world currency, and a return to commodity money like gold and silver to restore confidence.[271]

No serious thoughts are expressed in Washington about the Constitutional principle of local government.[272]

No matter how well-intended our militarism is portrayed, or how happily the promises of wonderful programs for the poor are promoted, inflating the money supply to pay these bills makes government bigger.[273]

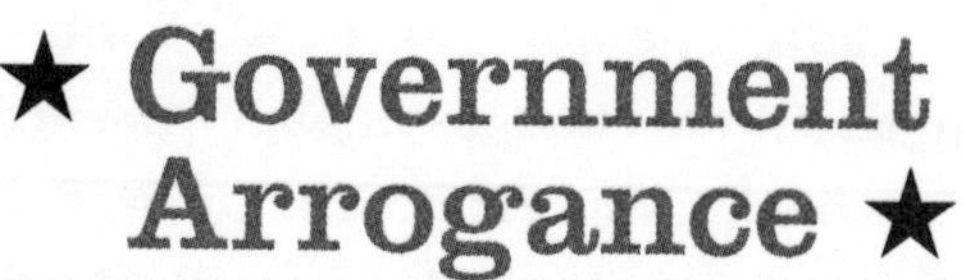

★ Government Arrogance ★

Lack of real choice in economic and personal decisions is commonplace. It seems that too often the only choice we're given is between prohibitions or subsidies. **Never is it said, "Let the people decide on things like stem cell research or alternative medical treatments."** [274]

Government Contracts

Those who are on the receiving end of government contracts—especially in the military-industrial complex during wartime—receive undeserved benefits.[275]

★

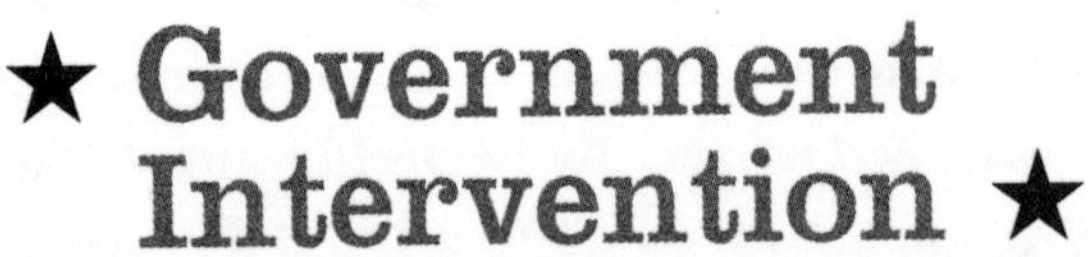

Government Intervention

Free market economics teaches that for every government action to solve an economic problem, two new ones are created. **The same unwanted results occur with foreign policy meddling.[276]**

★

The law of opposites is just a variation of the law of unintended consequences. When we attempt to achieve a certain goal—like, "make the world safe for democracy," a grandiose scheme of World War I—one can be sure the world will become less safe and less democratic regardless of the motivation.[277]

★ Habeas Corpus ★

Congress is not much better when it comes to protecting against the erosion of the centuries-old habeas corpus doctrine. By declaring anyone an "enemy combatant"–a totally arbitrary designation by the president–the government can deny an individual his right to petition a judge or even speak with an attorney. Though there has been a good debate on the insanity of our policy of torturing prisoners, holding foreigners and Americans without charges seems acceptable to many. Did it never occur to those who condemn torture that unlimited detention of individuals without a writ of habeas corpus is itself torture–especially for those who are totally innocent?[278]

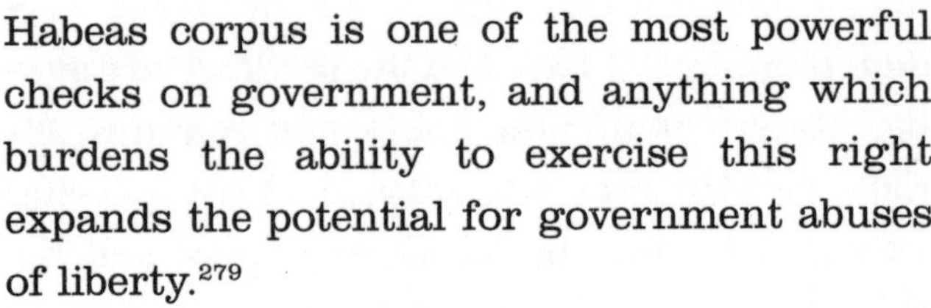

Habeas corpus is one of the most powerful checks on government, and anything which burdens the ability to exercise this right expands the potential for government abuses of liberty.[279]

I ask my colleagues to remember that in the centuries of experience with habeas corpus there is no evidence that it interferes with legitimate interests of law enforcement.[280]

★ Harry Browne ★

Mr. Speaker, America lost a great champion of liberty when Harry Browne passed away on March 1, at the age of seventy-two. Harry had a passion for liberty and knowledge of a wide variety of subjects. His communication style, as he himself so marvelously put it, focused on converting

his opponents rather than winning the argument. These attributes helped make him one of the most effective proponents of the freedom philosophy I have had the privilege of knowing. Harry's numerous books and columns, his radio and Internet broadcasts, and his speeches educated millions in sound economics and the benefits of a free society. Harry motivated many people to become activists in the movement to restore American liberties.[281]

★

★ Hate Crime Laws ★

Because federal hate crime laws criminalize thoughts, they are incompatible with a free society.[282]

★

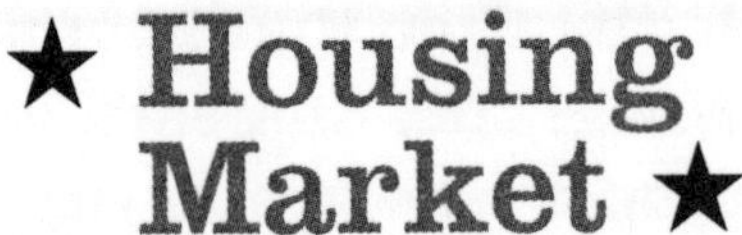

★ Housing Market ★

The implicit government backing of Fannie Mae and Freddie Mac [loan institutions] provides investors an incentive to provide funds to Fannie and Freddie that otherwise would have been put to use in other sectors of the economy. **It was this flood of investor capital that helped to fuel the housing bubble.**[283]

★ Immigration ★

Paper money, inflation, and the conditions they create contribute to the problems of illegal immigration.[284]

I remain very skeptical about the idea of so-called comprehensive immigration reform and the Senate compromise now being discussed. **I**

will oppose any legislation that in any way, shape, or form grants amnesty to the millions of people who are in this country illegally.[285]

Our current welfare system also encourages illegal immigration by discouraging American citizens to take low-wage jobs. This creates greater demand for illegal foreign labor. Welfare programs and minimum wage laws create an artificial market for labor to do the jobs Americans supposedly won't do.[286]

A sensible bill would bolster enforcement of existing immigration laws, reject any form of amnesty, and address the underlying welfare state that adds to the problem.[287]

Immigration admittedly is a difficult issue, and nobody wants America to become an unwelcoming fortress. **On the contrary, we need to attract the best and brightest people by remaining an entrepreneurial society that rewards initiative and hard work.**[288]

★ Income Tax ★

Accepting the principle behind both the income and the estate tax concedes the statist notion that the government owns the fruits of our labor, as well as our savings, and we are permitted by the politicians' "generosity" to keep a certain percentage. Every tax-cut proposal in Washington now is considered a "cost" to government, not the return of something rightfully belonging to a productive citizen. [289]

Inflation

Though runaway inflation is injurious to almost everyone, it is more insidious for certain groups. **Once inflation is recognized as a tax, it becomes clear the tax is regressive: penalizing the poor and middle class more than the rich and politically privileged.**[290]

Price inflation, a consequence of inflating the money supply by the central bank, hits poor and marginal workers first and foremost. It especially penalizes savers, retirees, those on fixed incomes, and anyone who trusts government promises.[291]

Inflation, as exposed by high gold prices, transfers wealth from the middle class to the rich, as real wages decline while the salaries of CEOs, movie stars, and athletes skyrocket—along with the profits of the military-industrial complex, the oil industry, and other special interests.[292]

Runaway inflation inevitably leads to political chaos, something numerous countries have suffered throughout the twentieth century. The worst example, of course, was the German inflation of the 1920s that led to the rise of Hitler. Even the communist takeover of China was associated with runaway inflation brought on by Chinese nationalists. The time for action is now, and it is up to the American people and the U.S. Congress to demand it.[293]

The tragedy is that the inflation tax is borne more by the poor and the middle class than the rich. Meanwhile, the well-connected rich, the politicians, the bureaucrats, the bankers, the military industrialists, and the international corporations reap the benefits of war profits.[294]

Government officials stick to their claim that no significant inflation exists, even as certain necessary costs are skyrocketing and incomes are stagnating.[295]

The Fed is solely responsible for inflation by creating money out of thin air.[296]

★ Inflation Tax ★

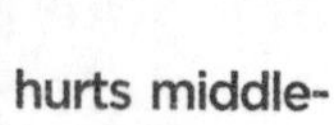

The inflation tax, while largely ignored, hurts middle-class and low-income Americans the most.[297]

If those who say they want to increase taxes to reduce the deficit got their way, who would benefit? No one! There's no historic evidence to show that taxing productive Americans to support both the rich and poor welfare beneficiaries helps the middle class, produces jobs, or stimulates the economy.[298]

★ Interest Rates ★

Interest rate manipulation by the central bank helps the rich, the banks, the government, and the politicians.[299]

The recent sharp rise in interest rates may well be signaling the end to the painless easy money decade that has allowed us to finance our extravagant welfare/warfare spending with minimal productive effort and no savings. **Monetary inflation and foreign borrowing have allowed us to live far beyond our means—a type of monetary arrangement that always comes to a painful end.**[300]

★ International Organizations ★

This unaccountable international organization is at the forefront of the manipulation

and meddling in the internal affairs of other sovereign states, and has repeatedly dishonored itself through politically biased monitoring of foreign elections. The Organization for Security and Cooperation in Europe (OSCE) does not deserve a penny from the American taxpayer, but this bill will make sure that the lavishly paid bureaucrats that staff the organization will be able to maintain their standard of living–at our expense.[301]

★

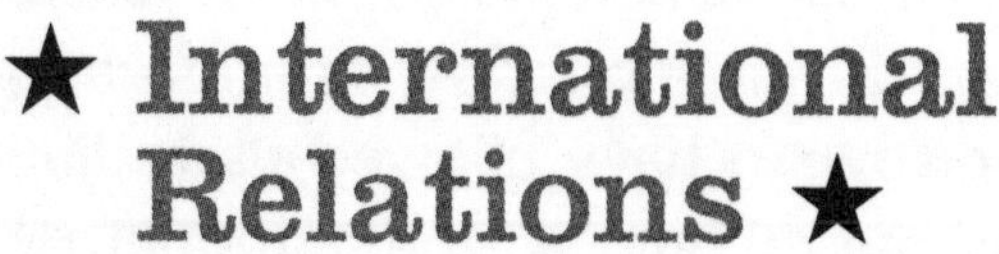

★ International Relations ★

If we treat other countries with respect and as equal partners, we might be pleased to find that our requests receive a more attentive ear. [302]

We forget that the weapons we feared Saddam Hussein had were supplied to him by the United States, and we refused to believe UN inspectors and the CIA that he no longer had them. Likewise, Iran received her first nuclear reactor from us. Now we're hysterically wondering if someday she might decide to build a bomb in self-interest.[303]

Pakistan has spread nuclear technology throughout the world, and in particular to the North Koreans. They flaunt international restrictions on nuclear weapons. But we reward them just as we reward India.[304]

★ Interventionism ★

We accommodated Iran by severely weakening the Taliban in Afghanistan on Iran's eastern borders. On Iran's western borders we helped the Iranians by eliminating their arch enemy, Saddam Hussein. Our invasion in Iraq and the resulting chaos have inadvertently delivered up a large portion of Iraq to the Iranians, as the majority Shiites in Iraq ally themselves with Iranians.[305]

The U.S./Israeli plan to hit Hezbollah in Lebanon before taking on Iran militarily has totally backfired. Now Hezbollah, an ally of Iran, has been made stronger than ever with the military failure to rout Hezbollah from southern Lebanon. Before the U.S./Israeli invasion of Lebanon, Hezbollah was supported by 20 percent of the population; now it's revered by 80 percent. A democratic election in Lebanon cannot now serve the interest of the United States or Israel. It would only support the cause of radical clerics in Iran.[306]

A foreign policy of interventionism costs so much money that we're forced to close military bases in the United States, even as we're building them overseas. **Interventionism is never good fiscal policy.**[307]

Interventionism symbolizes an attitude of looking outward, toward empire, while diminishing the importance of maintaining a Constitutional republic.[308]

This policy of interventionism is folly, and it cannot continue forever. It will end, either because we wake up or because we go broke.[309]

Interventionism always leads to unanticipated consequences and blowback, like: a weakened, demoralized military; exploding deficits; billions of dollars wasted; increased inflation; less economic growth; an unstable currency; painful stock market corrections; political demagoguery; lingering anger at home; and confusion about who is to blame. These elements combine to create an environment that inevitably undermines personal liberty. **Virtually all American wars have led to diminished civil liberties at home.**[310]

It seems of little concern to many members of Congress that we lack both the moral right and constitutional authority to impose our will on other nations.[311]

★ Iran ★

Our obsession with democracy–which is clearly conditional when one looks at our response to the recent Palestinian elections–will allow the majority Shia to claim leadership title if Iraq's election actually leads to an organized government. This delights the Iranians, who are close allies of the Iraqi Shia.[312]

I worry that before we can finish the war we're in and extricate ourselves, the patriotic fervor for expanding into Iran will drown out the cries of "enough already!"[313]

In the 1980s we provided weapons—including poisonous gas—to Saddam Hussein as we supported his invasion of Iran. These events are not forgotten by the Iranians, who see us once again looking for another confrontation with them. We insist that the UN ignore the guarantees under the NPT [Nuclear Non-Proliferation Treaty] that grant countries like Iran the right to enrich uranium. The pressure on the UN and the threats we cast toward Iran are quite harmful to the cause of peace. They are entirely unnecessary and serve no useful purpose. **Our policy toward Iran is much more likely to result in her getting a nuclear weapon than prevent it.**[314]

Our own effort at democratizing Iran has resulted instead in radicalizing a population whose instincts are to like Americans and our economic system. Our meddling these past fifty years has only served to alienate and unify the entire country against us.[315]

Though our officials only see Iran as an enemy, as does Israel, our policies in the Middle East these past five years have done wonders to strengthen Iran's political and military position in the region. We have totally ignored serious overtures by the Iranians to negotiate with us before hostilities broke out in Iraq in 2003. Both immediately after 9/11, and especially at the time of our invasion of Iraq in 2003, Iran, partially out of fear and realism, honestly sought reconciliation and offered to help the United States in its battle against al-Qaeda. They were rebuked outright. **Now Iran is negotiating from a much stronger position, principally as a result of our overall Middle East policy.**[316]

Iran has never in modern times invaded her neighbors, yet we worry obsessively that she may develop a nuclear weapon someday. Never mind that a radicalized Pakistan has nuclear weapons;

our friend Musharraf won't lift a finger against bin Laden, who most likely is hiding there. Our only defense against this emerging nuclear threat has been to use, and threaten to use, weapons that do not meet the needs of this new and different enemy.[317]

The moral of the story, Mr. Speaker, is this: **If you don't have a nuke, we'll threaten to attack you. If you do have a nuke, we'll leave you alone. In fact, we'll probably subsidize you.** What makes us think Iran does not understand this?[318]

We need to engage the rest of the world, including Iran and Syria, through diplomacy, trade, and travel rather than pass threatening legislation like this that paves the way to war.[319]

Clearly, language threatening to wipe a nation or a group of people off the map is to be condemned by all civilized people. And I do condemn any such language. But why does threatening Iran with a preemptive nuclear strike, as many here have done, not also deserve the same kind of condemnation?[320]

Our policies toward Iran have been more provocative than those towards Iraq. Yes, President Bush labeled Iran part of the axis of evil and unnecessarily provoked their anger at us. But **our mistakes with Iran started a long time before this president took office.**[321]

In 1953 our CIA, with help of the British, participated in overthrowing the democratic elected leader, Mohamed Mosaddeq. We placed the shah in power. He ruled ruthlessly but protected our oil interests, and for that we protected him—that is until 1979. We even provided him with

Iran's first nuclear reactor. Evidently we didn't buy the argument that his oil supplies precluded a need for civilian nuclear energy. From 1953 to 1979 his authoritarian rule served to incite a radical Muslim opposition led by the Ayatollah Khomeini, who overthrew the shah and took our hostages in 1979. This blowback event was slow in coming, but Muslims have long memories. The hostage crisis and overthrow of the shah by the ayatollah [were] a major victory for the radical Islamists. **Most Americans either never knew about or easily forgot our unwise meddling in the internal affairs of Iran in 1953.**[322]

Hysterical fear of Iran is way out of proportion to reality.[323]

During the 1980s we further antagonized Iran by supporting the Iraqis in their invasion of Iran.

This made our relationship with Iran worse, while sending a message to Saddam Hussein that invading a neighboring country is not all that bad. When Hussein got the message from our State Department that his plan to invade Kuwait was not of much concern to the United States, he immediately proceeded to do so. We in a way encouraged him to do it almost like we encouraged him to go into Iran. Of course this time our reaction was quite different, and all of a sudden our friendly ally Saddam Hussein became our arch enemy. The American people may forget this flip-flop, but those who suffered from it never forget. And the Iranians remember well our meddling in their affairs. Labeling the Iranians part of the axis of evil further alienated them and contributed to the animosity directed toward us.[324]

The sad truth is that the supposed dangers posed by Iran are no more real than those claimed about Iraq.[325]

There is no evidence of a threat to us by Iran, and no reason to plan and initiate a confrontation with her. **There are many reasons not to do so, however.**[326]

It's a bad idea.[327]

There's great danger in doing it.[328]

The whole world is against it.[329]

The plan is a hysterical reaction to a problem that does not yet exist.[330]

If it's carried out, the Middle East, and possibly the world, will explode.[331]

Oil will soar to over $100 a barrel, and gasoline will be over $5 a gallon.[332]

★ Iraq ★

The invasion of Iraq in 2003 was hyped as a noble mission, justified by misrepresentations of intelligence concerning Saddam Hussein and his ability to attack us and his neighbors.[333]

When people see a $600 million embassy being built in Baghdad, while funding for services here in the United States is hard to obtain, they become angry.[334]

★

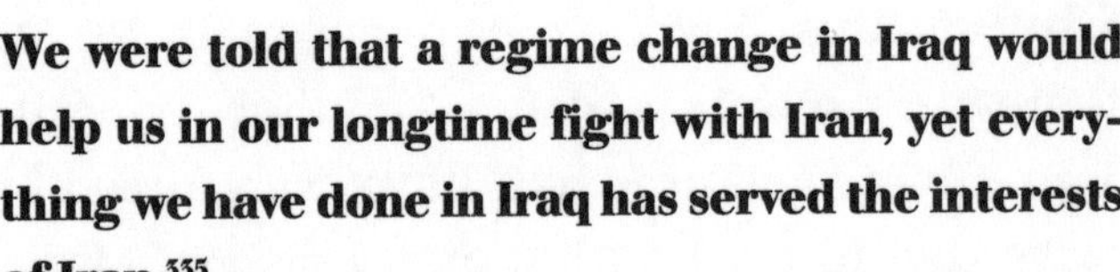

We were told that a regime change in Iraq would help us in our longtime fight with Iran, yet everything we have done in Iraq has served the interests of Iran.[335]

We're being told in a threatening and intimidating fashion that, "If America were to pull out before Iraq could defend itself, the consequences would be absolutely predictable and absolutely disastrous." **I'm convinced that the law of opposites could well apply here. Going into Iraq we know produced exactly the opposite results of what was predicted: Leaving also likely will have results opposite of those we're being frightened with.** Certainly leaving Vietnam at the height of the Cold War did not result in the disaster predicted by the advocates of the Domino Theory—an inevitable Communist takeover of the entire Far East.[336]

In our attempt to make Iraq a better place, we did great harm to Iraqi Christians. Before our invasion in 2003, there were approximately 1.2 million living in Iraq. Since then over half have been forced to leave due to persecution and violence. Many escaped to Syria. With the neocons wanting to attack Syria, how long will they be safe there? The answer to the question, "Aren't we better off without Saddam Hussein," is not an automatic yes for Iraqi Christians.[337]

In attempting to build an artificial and unwelcome Iraqi military, the harder we try, the more money we spend, and the more lives we lose, the stronger the real armies of Iraq become: the Sunni insurgency, the Bardr Brigade, the Sardr Mahdi Army, and the Kurdish militia.[338]

The Kurds have already taken a bold step in this direction by hoisting a Kurdish flag and removing the Iraqi flag—a virtual declaration of independence. **Natural local forces are winning out over outside political forces.**[339]

We're looking in all the wrong places for an Iraqi army to bring stability to that country. The people have spoken and these troops that represent large segments of the population need no training. It's not a lack of training, weapons, or money that hinders our efforts to create a new superior Iraqi military. **It's the lack of inspiration and support for such an endeavor that is missing.**[340]

Astonishingly, American taxpayers now will be forced to finance a multibillion dollar jobs program in Iraq. Suddenly the war is about jobs![341]

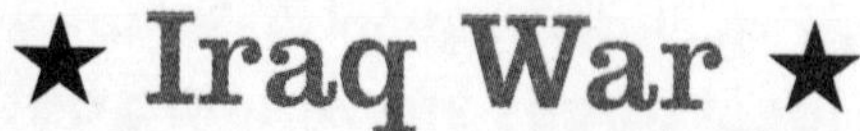

★ Iraq War ★

It's time to come home from Iraq, time to end the war.[342]

One of the reasons we went into Iraq was to secure "our" oil. **Before the Iraq war oil was less than $30 per barrel; today it is over $70.**[343]

Talk about unintended consequences! This war has produced chaos, civil war, death and destruction, and huge financial costs. It has eliminated two of Iran's worst enemies and placed power in Iraq with Iran's best friends. Even this apparent failure of policy does nothing to restrain the current march toward a similar confrontation with Iran. What will it take for us to learn from our failures?[344]

The anger over the Iraq war is multifaceted. Some are angry, believing they were lied to in order to gain their support at the beginning. Others are angry that the forty billion dollars we spend every year on intelligence gathering failed to provide good information. Proponents of the war too often are unable to admit the truth. **They become frustrated with the progress of the war and then turn on those wanting to change course, angrily denouncing them as unpatriotic and un-American.**[345]

Don't believe for a minute that additional congressional funding is needed so our troops can defend themselves or extricate themselves from the war zone. That's nonsense. **The Department of Defense has hundreds of billions of dollars in the pipeline available to move troops anywhere on earth—including home.**[346]

Resorting to a medical analogy, a wrong diagnosis was made at the beginning of the war and the wrong treatment was prescribed. Refusing to reassess our mistakes and insist on just more and more of a failed remedy is destined to kill the patient–in this case the casualties will be our liberties and prosperity here at home and peace abroad.[347]

The claim that it's unpatriotic to oppose spending more money in Iraq must be laid to rest as fraudulent.[348]

Congress failed to meet its responsibilities four years ago, unconstitutionally transferring its explicit war power to the executive branch. Even though the administration started the subsequent preemptive war in Iraq, **Congress bears the greatest responsibility for its lack of courage in fulfilling its duties.** Since then Congress has obediently provided the funds and troops required to pursue this illegitimate war.[349]

We won't solve the problems in Iraq until we confront our failed policy of foreign interventionism.[350]

Here's a new approach: Congress should admit its mistake and repeal the authority wrongfully given to the executive branch in 2002. Repeal the congressional sanction and disavow presidential discretion in starting wars. Then start bringing our troops home.[351]

The constant refrain that bringing our troops home would demonstrate a lack of support for them must be one of the most amazing distortions ever foisted on the American public. We're so concerned about saving face, but whose face are we saving? A sensible policy would save

American lives and follow the rules laid out for Congress in the Constitution—and avoid wars that have no purpose.[352]

If one is unhappy with our progress in Iraq after four years of war, voting to de-fund the war makes sense. If one is unhappy with the manner in which we went to war, without a Constitutional declaration, voting no makes equally good sense.[353]

Congress failed miserably in meeting its crucial obligations as the branch of government charged with deciding whether to declare war. It wrongly and unconstitutionally transferred this power to the president, and the president did not hesitate to use it.[354]

Congress bears the greater blame for this fiasco. It reneged on its responsibility to declare or not declare war. **It transferred this**

decision-making power to the executive branch and gave open sanction to anything the president did.[355]

As an Air Force officer serving from 1963–1968, I heard the same agonizing pleas from the American people. These pleas were met with the same excuses about why we could not change a deeply flawed policy and rethink the war in Vietnam. That bloody conflict, also undeclared and unconstitutional, seems to have taught us little despite the horrific costs.[356]

Once again, though everyone now accepts that the original justifications for invading Iraq were not legitimate, we are given excuses for not leaving. We flaunt our power by building permanent military bases and an enormous billion-dollar embassy, yet claim we have no plans to stay in Iraq permanently. Assurances that our presence in Iraq has nothing to do with oil are not believed in the Middle East.[357]

The argument for staying—to prevent civil war and bring stability to the region—logically falls on deaf ears. If the justifications for war were wrong; if the war is going badly; if we can't afford the costs, both human and economic; if civil war and chaos have resulted from our occupation; if the reasons for staying are no more credible than the reasons for going; then . . . why the dilemma? **The American people have spoken, and continue to speak out, against this war. So why not end it?**[358]

More good things may come of it than anyone can imagine. Consider our relationship with Vietnam, now our friendly trading partner. Certainly we are doing better with her than when we tried to impose our will by force. It is time to march out of Iraq and march home.[359]

Congress's job is to change the policy on Iraq, not to tell the military leaders how many troops they should have.[360]

Clearly the American public is overwhelmingly in favor of a withdrawal from Iraq, but Congress is not listening. At best, the House seems willing to consider only such half-measures as so-called redeployment. We need a real solution that puts the safety of our troops above politics. We need to simply bring them home. As I said recently on the floor of the House, we just marched in, so we can just march out.[361]

The argument in Washington is over tactics, quality of intelligence, war management, and diplomacy, except for the few who admit that tragic mistakes were made and now sincerely want to establish a new course for Iraq.[362]

Ironically, our involvement has produced an unusual agreement among the Kurds, Shiites, and Sunnis, the three factions at odds with each other. At the recent twenty-two-member Arab League meeting in Cairo, the three groups agreed on one issue: **They all want foreign troops to leave.**[363]

It is a serious error to conclude that "fighting them over there" keeps them from fighting us "over here," or that we're winning the war against terrorism. As long as our occupation continues, and American forces continue killing Muslims, the incentive to attack us will grow.[364]

By limiting the debate to technical points over intelligence, strategy, the number of troops, and how to get out of the mess, we ignore our continued policy of sanctions, threats, and intimidation of Iraq's neighbors, Iran and Syria. **Even as Congress pretends to argue about**

how or when we might come home, leaders from both parties continue to support the policy of spreading the war by precipitating a crisis with these two countries.[365]

The likelihood of agreeing about who deliberately or innocently misled Congress, the media, and the American people is virtually nil. Maybe historians at a later date will sort out the whole mess.[366]

The decision to go to war is profound. It behooves Congress to ask more questions and investigate exactly how the president, Congress, and the people were misled into believing that invading Iraq was necessary for our national security.[367]

Supporters of the war in Iraq, as well as some nonsupporters, warn of the dangers if we leave.

But isn't it quite possible that these dangers are simply a consequence of having gone into Iraq in the first place, rather than a consequence of leaving? Isn't it possible that staying only makes the situation worse? **If chaos results after our departure, it's because we occupied Iraq, not because we left.**[368]

Civil strife, if not civil war, already exists in Iraq—and despite the infighting, all factions oppose our occupation.[369]

Though most people think this war started in March of 2003, the seeds were sown many years before. The actual military conflict, involving U.S. troops against Iraq, began in January 1991. The prelude to this actually dates back over a hundred years, when the value of Middle East oil was recognized by the industrialized West.[370]

It's virtually impossible to beat a determined guerrilla resistance to a foreign occupying force. After thirty years the Vietnam guerrillas, following unbelievable suffering, succeeded in forcing all foreign troops from their homeland. History shows that Iraqi Muslims have always been determined to resist any foreign power on their soil. We ignored that history and learned nothing from Vietnam. **How many lives, theirs and ours, are worth losing to prove the tenacity of guerrilla fighters supported by a large number of local citizens?**[371]

There were no weapons of mass destruction, no biological or chemical or nuclear weapons, so we can be assured the Iraqis pose no threat to anyone, certainly not to the United States.[372]

The claim that our immediate withdrawal from Iraq would cause chaos is not proven. It didn't happen in Vietnam or even Somalia. Even today, the

militias of the Kurds and the Shiites may well be able to maintain order in their regions much better than we can currently. Certainly the Sunnis can take care of themselves, and it might be in their best interests for all three groups not to fight each other when we leave. **One thing [is] for sure: If we left, no more young Americans would have to die for an indefinable cause.**[373]

Islamic Fanaticism

The Islamic fascists are almost impossible to identify and cannot be targeted by our conventional weapons. Those who threaten us essentially are unarmed and stateless. Comparing them to Nazi Germany, a huge military power, is ridiculous. Labeling them as a unified force is a mistake. It's critical that we figure out why a growing number of Muslims are radicalized to the point of committing suicide terrorism against us. **Our presence in their countries represents a failed policy that makes us less safe, not more.**[374]

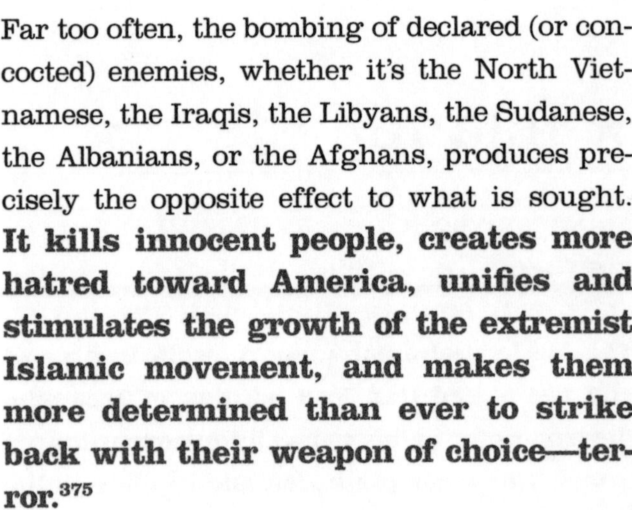

Far too often, the bombing of declared (or concocted) enemies, whether it's the North Vietnamese, the Iraqis, the Libyans, the Sudanese, the Albanians, or the Afghans, produces precisely the opposite effect to what is sought. **It kills innocent people, creates more hatred toward America, unifies and stimulates the growth of the extremist Islamic movement, and makes them more determined than ever to strike back with their weapon of choice—terror.**[375]

Our current policy in the Middle East is indeed a threat to our security, for it puts more Americans in increased danger. **Protecting our so-called interests, that is, controlling Arab oil, is not worth the danger of giving the Islamic extremist the ammunition and the incentive to unite an entire region—a region that quite possibly has access to nuclear**

weapons—against all American citizens around the world.[376]

★ Islamic State ★

So far our policies inadvertently have encouraged the development of an Islamic state, with Iranian-allied Shiites in charge. This has led to Iranian support for the insurgents and has placed Iran in a position of becoming the true victor in this war as its alliance with Iraq grows. This could place Iran and its allies in the enviable position of becoming the oil powerhouse in the region, if not the world, once it has control over the oil fields near Basra.[377]

Our bombs and guns haven't changed the fact that the new puppet Afghan government still follows Sharia law. The same loyalty to Sharia exists in Iraq, where we're trying so hard to stabilize things. **And all this is done in the name of spreading democracy.**[378]

★ Israel ★

We've been told for decades that our policy of militarism and preemption in the Middle East is designed to provide security for Israel. Yet a very strong case can be made that Israel is more vulnerable than ever, with moderate Muslims being challenged by a growing majority of Islamic radicals. **As the invincibility of the American and Israeli military becomes common knowledge, Israel's security is diminished and world opinion turns against her, especially after the failed efforts to remove the Hezbollah threat.**[379]

We were told that attacking and eliminating Hezbollah was required to diminish the Iranian threat against Israel. The results again were the opposite. **This failed effort has only emboldened Iran.**[380]

Behind the scenes many were quite aware that Israel's influence on our foreign policy played a role. She had argued for years, along with the neoconservatives, for an Iraqi regime change. This support was nicely coordinated with the Christian Zionists' enthusiasm for the war.[381]

This unintended alliance with Iran, plus the benefit to Osama bin Laden's recruiting efforts, will in the end increase the danger to Israel by rallying the Arab and Muslim people against us.[382]

★ Lebanon ★

Remember, once we left Lebanon, suicide terrorism stopped and peace finally came. The same could happen in Iraq.[383]

★ Liberty ★

Whether it's the extraction of wealth from the productive economy, the distortion of the market by interest rate manipulation, or spending for war and welfare, it can't happen without infringing upon personal liberty.[384]

There's no reason to sacrifice liberty in thinking that you're going to be safer.[385]

With no consistent moral defense of true liberty, the continued erosion of personal and property rights is inevitable.[386]

Congress could promote both liberty and security by encouraging private property owners to take more responsibility to protect themselves and their property.[387]

A government that is willing to enslave some of its people can never be trusted to protect the liberties of its own citizens.[388]

★ Lobbyists ★

As long as the federal government continues to regulate, tax, and subsidize the American people, there will be attempts to influence those who write the laws and regulations under which the people must live.[389]

Human nature being what it is, there will also be those lobbyists and policy makers who manipulate the power of the regulatory state to enrich themselves.[390]

Instead of passing new regulations and laws regulating the people's right to petition their government, **my colleagues should refuse**

to vote for any legislation that violates the Constitutional limits on federal power or enriches a special interest at the expense of American taxpayers.[391]

Today though, any new rules designed to restrain special interest favoritism will only push the money further under the table. Too much is at stake.[392]

The problem of special-interest government that breeds corruption comes from our lack of respect for the Constitution in the first place. So what do we do? **We further violate the Constitution rather than examine it for guidance as to the proper role of the federal government.**[393]

Laws addressing bribery, theft, and fraud, already on the books, are adequate to deal with the criminal activities associated with lobbying. New laws and regulations are unnecessary.[394]

★ Martial Law ★

Now, martial law can be declared not just for "insurrection" but also for "natural disasters, public health reasons, terrorist attacks or incidents," or for the vague reason called "other conditions." The president can call up the National Guard without Congressional approval or the governors' approval and even send these state guard troops into other states.[395]

Most would associate military patrols, martial law, and summary executions with a police state, something obviously not present in our everyday activities. However, those with knowledge of Ruby Ridge, Mount Carmel, and other such incidents may have a different opinion.[396]

★ Media ★

Politics as usual is aided by the complicity of the media. Economic ignorance, bleeding heart emotionalism, and populist passion pervade our major networks and cable channels. This is especially noticeable when the establishment seeks to unify the people behind an illegal, unwise war. **The propaganda is well coordinated by the media/government/military-industrial complex.**[397]

The liberal mainstream media also benefit from campaign finance restrictions. When lobbies and individuals are limited in what they can give to campaigns and political parties, they instead will spend money on advertisements during election seasons. Media outlets relish the prospect of increased ad revenue.[398]

A strong undercurrent of dissent has manifested itself below the mainstream media radar, on radio talk shows and Web sites.[399]

Why should giant media companies be able to spend unlimited amounts of money to promote candidates and issues, while an organization you support cannot? The notion of creating a preferred class of media, with special First Amendment rights, is distinctly elitist and un-American.[400]

★ Medical Privacy ★

Instead of further eroding our medical privacy, Congress should take steps to protect it. Why should someone be prevented from denying the government and third parties access to his medical records without his permission or a warrant?[401]

One way the House can act to protect patients' privacy is by enacting my Patient Privacy Act (HR 1699) that repeals the provision of federal law establishing a medical ID for every American.[402]

Under the guise of "protecting privacy," the Health and Human Services' so-called "medical privacy" regulations allow medical researchers, insurance agents, and government officials access to your personal medical records—without your consent! **Congress should act now to reverse this government-imposed invasion of our medical privacy.**[403]

★

Middle East ★

I smell an expanded war in the Middle East, and pray that I'm wrong. I sense that circumstances will arise that demand support regardless of the danger and cost. **Any lack of support, once again, will be painted as being soft on**

terrorism and al-Qaeda. We will be told we must support Israel, support patriotism, support the troops, and defend freedom.[404]

Our failed efforts in Iraq continue to drain our resources, costing us dearly both in lives lost and dollars spent. And there's no end in sight. No consideration is given for rejecting our obsession with a worldwide military presence, which rarely if ever directly enhances our security.[405]

Both sides of the war in the Middle East are driven by religious beliefs of omnipotence. Both sides endorse an eschatological theory regarding the forthcoming end of time. Both anticipate the return of God personified and as promised to each. Both sides are driven by a conviction of perfect knowledge regarding the Creator, and though we supposedly worship the same God, each sees the other side as completely wrong and blasphemous. The religiously driven Middle East war condemns tolerance of the other's view. **Advocates of restraint and the use of diplomacy are ridiculed as appeasers, and equivalent to supporting Nazism and considered un-American and un-Christian.**[406]

Being falsely accused of anti-Semitism and being a supporter of radical fascism is not an enviable position for any politician. **Most realize it's best to be quiet and support our Middle East involvement.**[407]

★ Militarism ★

The lack of success of conventional warfare—the United States in Vietnam, the Soviets in Afghanistan, the United States in Iraq and Afghanistan, Israel in Lebanon—should awaken our policy makers to our failure in war and diplomacy. **Yet all we propose are bigger bombs and more military force**

for occupation, rather than working to understand an entirely new generation of modern warfare.[408]

Many reasons are given for our preemptive wars and military approach for spreading the American message of freedom and prosperity, which is an obvious impossibility. Our vital interests are always cited for justification, and it's inferred that those who do not support our militancy are unpatriotic. Yet the opposite is actually the case: **Wise resistance to one's own government doing bad things requires a love of country, devotion to idealism, and respect for the rule of law.**[409]

We have a troop shortage, morale is low, and our military equipment is in bad shape, yet the neocons would not hesitate to spend, borrow, inflate, and reinstate the draft to continue their grandiose schemes in remaking the entire

Middle East. **Obviously a victory of this sort is not available, no matter what effort is made or how much money is spent.**[410]

The real reason for our militarism is rarely revealed and hidden from the public.[411]

The twentieth century has truly been a century of unbelievable technological advancement. We should be cognizant of what this technology has done to the size and nature of our own government. It could easily be argued that, with greater technological advances, the need for government ought to decline and private alternatives be enhanced. But there's not much evidence for that argument. In 1902 the cost of government activities at all levels came to 7.7 percent of the gross domestic product; today it's more than 50 percent.[412]

★ Military Commissions Act ★

The Military Commissions Act gives unconscionable powers to the executive branch—secret military commissions, torture, arbitrary detention of American citizens, warrantless searches, imprisonment based on secret testimony. **It's not just unconstitutional; it's actually an assault on the principles that underlie our republic.**[413]

The Military Commissions Act is a particularly egregious piece of legislation and, if not repealed, will change America for the worse as the powers unconstitutionally granted to the executive branch are used and abused. [414]

This act grants excessive authority to use secretive military commissions outside of places where active hostilities are going on.[415]

The Military Commissions Act permits torture, arbitrary detention of American citizens as unlawful enemy combatants at the full discretion of the president and without the right of habeas corpus, and warrantless searches by the National Security Agency.[416]

★

★ Military Intervention ★

It's amazing what ending military intervention in the affairs of others can achieve. **Setting an example of how a free market economy works does wonders.**[417]

There has been some discontent among conservatives about the twenty billion dollar reconstruction price tag. They fail to realize that this is just the other side of the coin of military interventionism. It is the same coin, which is why I have consistently opposed foreign interventionism.[418]

The real point is that the billions we are told we must spend to rebuild Iraq [are] indeed the natural outcome of our policy of preemptive military intervention.[419]

Conservatives often proclaim that they are opposed to providing American welfare to the rest of the world. I agree. The only way to do that, however, is to stop supporting a policy of military interventionism. You cannot have one without the other.[420]

★ Military Victory ★

Mr. Speaker, a military victory in Iraq is unattainable, just as it was in the Vietnam War.[421]

At the close of the Vietnam War in 1975, a telling conversation took place between a North Vietnamese Army colonel named Tu and an American colonel named Harry Summers. Colonel Summers reportedly said, "You never beat us on the battlefield." Tu replied, "That may be so, but it is also irrelevant." **It is likewise irrelevant to seek military victory in Iraq.**[422]

Will the euphoria of grand military victories—against non-enemies—ever be mellowed? Someday, we as a legislative body must face the reality of the dire situation in which we have allowed ourselves to become enmeshed. Hopefully, it will be soon![423]

★ Minimum Wage ★

I would ask my colleagues, if the minimum wage is the means to prosperity, why stop at $6.65—why not $50, $75, or $100 per hour?[424]

Those who are denied employment opportunities as a result of the minimum wage are often young people at the lower end of the income scale who are seeking entry-level employment. Their inability to find an entry-level job will limit their employment prospects for years to come. Thus, **raising the minimum wage actually lowers the employment and standard of living of the very people proponents of the minimum wage claim will benefit from government intervention in the economy!**[425]

★ Money Growth ★

Since 1997 the world money supply has doubled. And money growth is inflation, which is the enemy of the poor and the middle class but a friend to the banks and Wall Street.[426]

★ Nation Building ★

Many reasons have been given for why we fight and our youth must die in Iraq. The reasons now given for why we must continue this war bear no resemblance to the reasons given to gain the support of the American people and the United States Congress prior to our invasion in March of 2003. Before the war, we were told we faced an imminent threat to our national security from Saddam Hussein. This rationale, now proven grossly mistaken, has been changed. Now we're told we must honor the fallen by "completing the mission." To do otherwise would demean the sacrifice of those who have died or been wounded. Any lack of support for "completing the mission" is said, by the promoters of the war, to be unpatriotic, un-American, and detrimental to the troops. They insist the only way one can support the troops is to never waver on the policy of nation building,

no matter how ill-founded that policy may be. The obvious flaw in this argument is that the mission, of which they so reverently speak, has changed constantly from the very beginning.[427]

The pervasive and indefinable enemy—terrorism—cannot be conquered with weapons and UN nation building—only a more sensible pro-American foreign policy will accomplish this. This must occur if we are to avoid a cataclysmic expansion of the current hostilities.[428]

The president, in the 2000 presidential campaign, argued against nation building, and he was right to do so. He also said, "If we're an arrogant nation, they'll resent us." He wisely argued for humility and a policy that promotes peace.[429]

Our obsession with policing the world, nation building, and preemptive war are not likely to soon go away, since both Republican and Democratic leaders endorse them.[430]

★

★ National Criminal Background System ★

Among the information that must be submitted to the database are medical, psychological, and drug treatment records that have traditionally been considered protected from disclosure under the physician-patient relationship, as well as records related to misdemeanor domestic violence.[431]

★

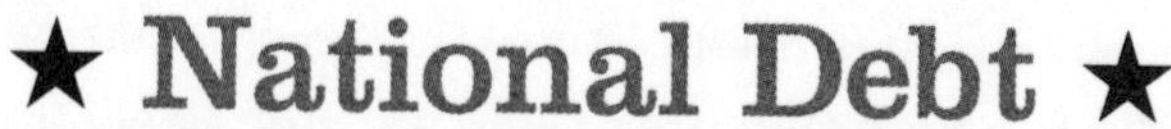

★ National Debt ★

It doesn't take a genius to realize that increasing the national debt by over $600 billion per year is not sustainable.[432]

★ National ID ★

A national ID card is now in the process of being implemented. It's called the Real ID card, and it's tied to our Social Security numbers and our state driver's license. **If Real ID is not stopped, it will become a national driver's license/ID for all America.**[433]

Nationalizing standards for drivers' licenses and birth certificates, and linking them together via a national database, creates a national ID system pure and simple. Proponents of the national ID understand that the public remains wary of the scheme, so they attempt to claim they're merely creating new standards for existing state IDs. Nonsense! This legislation imposes federal standards in a federal bill, and it creates a federalized ID regardless of whether the ID itself is still stamped with the name of your state. It is just a matter of time until those who refuse to carry the new licenses will be denied the ability to drive or board an airplane. **Domestic travel restrictions are the hallmark of authoritarian states, not free republics.**[434]

The national ID will be used to track the movements of American citizens, not just terrorists. Subjecting every citizen to surveillance actually diverts resources away from tracking and apprehending terrorists in favor of needless snooping on innocent Americans.[435]

Neoconservative

The neoconservative instigators of the war are angry at everyone: at the people who want to get out of Iraq, and especially at those prosecuting the war for not bombing more aggressively, sending in more troops, and expanding the war into Iran.[436]

For whatever reasons the neoconservatives might give, they are bound and determined to confront the Iranian government and demand changes in its leadership. This policy will further spread our military presence and undermine our security.[437]

Let there be no doubt: The neoconservative warriors are still in charge, and are conditioning Congress, the media, and the American people for a preemptive attack on Iran. Never mind that Afghanistan has unraveled and Iraq is in civil war: Serious plans

are being laid for the next distraction, which will further spread this war in the Middle East.[438]

The top neocon of the twentieth century was Woodrow Wilson. His supposed idealism, symbolized in the slogan "Make the world safe for democracy," resulted in untold destruction and death across the world for many decades. His deceit and manipulation of the prewar intelligence from Europe dragged America into an unnecessary conflict that cost the world and us dearly. Without the disastrous Versailles Treaty, World War II could have been averted—and the rise to power of Communists around the world might have been halted.[439]

We seem to never learn from our past mistakes. Today's neocons are as idealistically misled and aggressive in remaking the Middle East as the Wilsonian do-gooders. Even given the horrendous costs of the Iraq war and the unintended consequences that plague us today, **the neocons are eager to expand their regime-change policy to Iran by force.**[440]

Finally, after years of plotting and maneuvering, the neoconservative plan to invade Iraq came before the U.S. House in October 2002 to be rubber-stamped. Though the plan was hatched years before, and the official policy of the United States government was to remove Saddam Hussein ever since 1998, various events delayed the vote until this time. By October the vote was deemed urgent, so as to embarrass anyone who opposed it. This would make them politically vulnerable in the November election. The ploy worked. The resolution passed easily, and it served the interests of proponents of war in the November election.[441]

Reagan's willingness to admit error and withdraw from Lebanon was heroic and proved to be life-saving. True to form, many neocons with their love of war exude contempt for Reagan's decision. To them force and violence are heroic, not reassessing a bad situation and changing policy accordingly.[442]

★ Noninterventionism ★

When goals are couched in terms of humanitarianism, sincere or not, the results are inevitably bad. Foreign interventionism requires the use of force. First, the funds needed to pursue a particular policy require that taxes be forcibly imposed on the American people, either directly or indirectly through inflation. Picking sides in foreign countries only increases the chances of antagonism toward us. Too often foreign economic and military support means impoverishing the poor in America and enhancing the rich ruling classes in poor countries.[443]

Even Congress is deceived into supporting adventurism they would not accept if fully informed.[444]

A foreign policy of intervention invites all kinds of excuses for spreading ourselves around the world. The debate shifts from nonintervention versus interventionism, to where and for what particular reason should we involve ourselves. Most of the time it's for less than honorable reasons. **Even when cloaked in honorable slogans—like making the world safe for democracy—the unintended consequences and the ultimate costs cancel out the good intentions.**[445]

Conservatives, libertarians, Constitutionalists, and many of today's liberals have all at one time or another endorsed a less interventionist foreign policy. There's no reason a coalition of these groups might not once again present the case for a pro-American, nonmilitant, noninterventionist foreign policy dealing with all nations.[446]

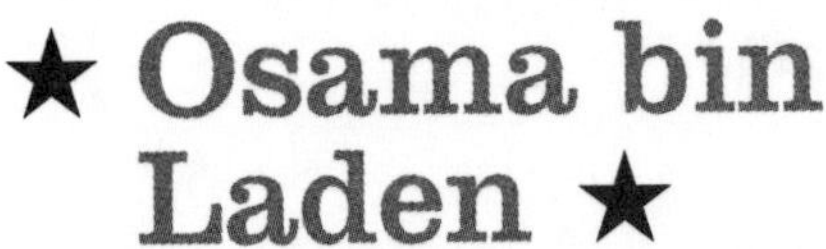

★ Osama bin Laden ★

Osama bin Laden has expressed sadistic pleasure with our invasion of Iraq and was surprised that we served his interests above and beyond his dreams on how we responded after the 9/11 attacks. His pleasure comes from our policy of folly getting ourselves bogged down in the middle of a religious civil war, 7,000 miles from home that is financially bleeding us to death. Total costs now are reasonably estimated to exceed $2 trillion. His recruitment of Islamic extremists has been greatly enhanced by our occupation of Iraq.[447]

Many experts believe bin Laden welcomed our invasion and occupation of two Muslim countries. It bolsters his claim that the United States intended to occupy and control the Middle East all along. This has galvanized radical

Muslim fundamentalists against us. **Osama bin Laden's campaign surely would suffer if we left.**[448]

Would an attack on Iraq not just confirm the Arab world's worst suspicions about the United States, and isn't this what bin Laden wanted?[449]

★ Pakistan ★

Following the September 11 disasters, a militant Islamic group in Pakistan held up a sign for all the world to see. It said: Americans, think! Why you are hated all over the world. We abhor the messenger, but we should not ignore the message.[450]

In the name of clamping down on "terrorist uprisings" in Pakistan, General Musharraf has declared a state of emergency and imposed martial law. The true motivations behind this action, however, are astonishingly transparent, as the reports come in that mainly lawyers and opposition party members are being arrested and harassed. Supreme Court justices are held in house arrest after indicating some reluctance to certify the legitimacy of Musharraf's recent reelection.[451]

Meanwhile, terrorist threats on U.S. interests may be more likely to originate from Pakistan, a country to which we have sent $10 billion.[452]

Now we are placed in the difficult position of either continuing to support a military dictator, who has taken some blatantly undemocratic courses of action, or withdrawing support and angering this nuclear-capable country.[453]

★ Partisan Politics ★

Though there's little difference between the two parties, the partisan fights are real. Instead of debates about philosophy, the partisan battles are about who will wield the gavels. True policy debates are rare; power struggles are real and ruthless. And yet we all know that power corrupts.[454]

For too long now, we have seen partisan battles and displays of heightened rhetoric about who wants to provide the most assistance to education distract us from our important work of removing government-imposed barriers to educational excellence.[455]

On occasion I hear comments like "You just don't vote with the majority enough." Some cannot understand it when I vote with a small group of people or by myself. But when I talk to people in my district and tell them how I feel about a particular issue, I believe that I owe it to them to vote in Washington in a fashion that is consistent with what I tell them. **If I give my word to the people, I believe I must then vote the way I tell them that I will. This is what I must do even when it means that my votes will not be popular with politicians in Washington, even with some in my own political party.**[456]

★

★ Patriot Act ★

The accelerated attacks on liberty started quickly after 9/11. Within weeks the Patriot Act was overwhelmingly passed by Congress. Though the final version was unavailable up to a few hours before the vote—no member had sufficient time to read or understand it—**political fear of "not doing something," even something harmful, drove members of Congress to not question the contents and just vote for it.** A little less freedom for a little more perceived safety was considered a fair trade-off—and the majority of Americans applauded.[457]

The Patriot Act, though, severely eroded the system of checks and balances by giving the state the power to spy on law-abiding citizens without judicial supervision. The several provisions that undermine the liberties of all Americans include: sneak-and-peek searches; a broadened and more vague definition of domestic terrorism; allowing the FBI access to libraries and bookstore records without search warrants or probable cause; easier FBI initiation of wiretaps and searches, as well as roving wiretaps; easier access to information on American citizens' use of the Internet; and easier access to e-mail and financial records of all American citizens.[458]

The debate in Congress—if that's what one wants to call it—boils down to whether the most egregious parts of the act will be sunsetted after four years or seven. The conference report will adjust the numbers, and members will vote willingly for the "compromise" and feel good about their effort to protect individual privacy. But if we're honest with ourselves, we would admit that the Fourth Amendment is essentially a dead letter. There has been no effort to curb the abuse of national security letters nor to comprehend the significance of echelon. **Hard-fought liberties are rapidly slipping away from us.**[459]

Certainly the Patriot Act would have never been passed, because it wasn't available to us. . . . It was almost 400 pages long and became available less than an hour before it was debated on the House floor. . . . The Congress members were intimidated, "If I do nothing, my people are gonna be mad, because they want us to do something." And the people are frightened. When they are frightened, they are much more willing to give us their liberties. But giving up their liberties won't make them safer. That's the real sad part of it.[460]

★ Patriotism ★

Today we constantly hear innuendos and direct insults aimed at those who dare to challenge current foreign policy, no matter how flawed that policy may be. **I would suggest it takes more courage to admit the truth, to admit mistakes, than to attack others as unpatriotic for disagreeing with the war in Iraq.**[461]

For some, patriotism is "the last refuge of a scoundrel." For others, it means dissent against a government's abuse of the people's rights.[462]

Peaceful nonviolent revolutions against tyranny have been every bit as successful as those involving military confrontation. Mahatma Gandhi and Dr. Martin Luther King Jr. achieved great politi-

cal successes by practicing nonviolence, yet they themselves suffered physically at the hands of the state. But whether the resistance against government tyrants is nonviolent or physically violent, the effort to overthrow state oppression qualifies as true patriotism.[463]

Unquestioned loyalty to the state is especially demanded in times of war. Lack of support for a war policy is said to be unpatriotic. Arguments against a particular policy that endorses a war once started are always said to be endangering the troops in the field. This, they blatantly claim, is unpatriotic, and all dissent must stop. **Yet it is dissent from government policies that defines the true patriot and champion of liberty.**[464]

It is conveniently ignored that the only authentic way to best support the troops is to keep them out of dangerous, undeclared, no-win wars that are politically inspired. Sending troops off to war for reasons that are not truly related to national security—and for that matter may even damage our security—is hardly a way to "patriotically" support the troops.[465]

Out of fear of being labeled unpatriotic, most citizens become compliant and accept the argument that some loss of liberty is required to fight the war in order to remain safe. This is a bad trade-off in my estimation, especially when done in the name of patriotism.[466]

Once a war of any sort is declared, the message is sent out not to object or you will be declared unpatriotic.[467]

The true patriot challenges the state when the state embarks on enhancing its power at the expense of the individual. Without a better understanding and a greater determination to rein in the state, the rights of Americans that resulted from the revolutionary break from the British and the writing of the Constitution will disappear.[468]

★

★ Phil Crane ★

Mr. Speaker, I am pleased to take this opportunity to pay tribute to my friend and colleague Phil Crane. During his thirty-five years in Congress, Phil has been one of the House's most consistent defenders of low taxes, free markets, limited government, and individual liberty. I count myself among the numerous elected officials and activists in the free-market movement who have been inspired by his example.[469]

★

As a conservative professor, author, and activist, Phil was already a nationally known conservative

leader before he ran for Congress. Two of his books, *The Democrat's Dilemma* and *The Sum of Good Government* stand out as conservative classics that educated and motivated many conservative activists.[470]

★ Pledge of Allegiance ★

Mr. Speaker, I am pleased to support, and cosponsor, the Pledge Protection Act (HR 2028), which restricts federal court jurisdiction over the question of whether the phrase "under God" should be included in the Pledge of Allegiance.[471]

Local schools should determine for themselves whether or not students should say "under God" in the pledge.[472]

Ironically, the author of the Pledge of Allegiance might disagree with our commitment to preserving the prerogatives of state and local governments.[473]

Francis Bellamy, the author of the pledge, was a self-described socialist who wished to replace the founders' Constitutional republic with a strong, centralized welfare state. Bellamy wrote the pledge as part of his efforts to ensure that children put their allegiance to the central government before their allegiance to their families, local communities, state governments, and even their Creator! **In fact, the atheist Bellamy did not include the words "under God" in his original version of the pledge. That phrase was added to the pledge in the 1950s.**[474]

★

★ Presidential Restraint ★

How can I run for office and say I want to be a weak president? **We need a strong president,**

strong enough to resist the temptation of taking power the president shouldn't have. [475]

It isn't only our presidents that deserve the blame when they overstep their authority and lead the country into inappropriate wars. Congress deserves equally severe criticism for acquiescing to the demands of the executive to go needlessly to war. It has been known throughout history that kings, dictators, and the executive branch of governments are always overly eager to go to war. This is precisely why our founders tried desperately to keep decisions about going to war in the hands of the legislature. But this process has failed us for the last sixty-five years. **Congress routinely has rubber-stamped the plans of our presidents and even the United Nations to enter into war through the back door.**[476]

The president can set a tone for fiscal restraint or indulgence, and can veto spending bills if he has the political will to do so.[477]

★ Price Controls 

Goods which originally are affordable only by the very rich, over the course of time and because of the fall in prices will become available to the poor and the middle class, raising the standard of living of all Americans. One hundred years ago a rich person might have driven a car and a poor person would have walked barefoot. Today a rich person might drive a Lexus, while a poor person drives a Kia, but they both have cars, and shoes. Price stability attempts to disadvantage consumers by keeping prices stable, rather than allowing them to take their natural course of decline. **This policy comes from two misguided notions: that lower prices lead to lower profits, and that lower prices lead to deflation.[478]**

★ Protectionism ★

A sound economic process is disrupted with a war economy and monetary inflation. Strong voices emerge blaming the wrong policies for our problems, prompting an outcry for protectionist legislation. It's always easier to blame foreign producers and savers for our inflation, lack of savings, excess debt, and loss of industrial jobs. **Protectionist measures only make economic conditions worse. Inevitably these conditions, if not corrected, lead to a lower standard of living for most of our citizens.**[479]

It is no longer politically fashionable to ask for "protection" from foreign competition. Instead, they demand that supreme "virtue" of American politics: fairness.[480]

Tariffs are taxes, and imposing new tariffs means raising taxes.[481]

Tariffs reward the strongest Washington lobbies.[482]

★ Protest ★

Liberals, who withhold their taxes as a protest against war, are vilified as well–especially by conservative statists.[483]

America was born of protest, revolution, and mistrust of government.[484]

Yet, we must not forget that the true patriot is the one who protests in spite of the consequences, condemnation or ostracism, or even imprisonment that may result.[485]

Legitimate protest against the government could place you (and tens of thousands of other Americans) under federal surveillance.[486]

★ Racism ★

Racism is simply an ugly form of collectivism, the mind-set that views humans strictly as members of groups rather than individuals. Racists believe that all individuals who share superficial physical characteristics are alike: As collectivists, racists think only in terms of groups. **By encouraging Americans to adopt a group mentality, the advocates of so-called "diversity" actually perpetuate racism. Their obsession with racial group identity is inherently racist.** The true antidote to racism is liberty. Liberty means having a limited, Constitutional government devoted to the protection of individual rights rather than group claims. Liberty means free-market capitalism, which rewards individual achievement and competence, not skin color, gender, or ethnicity.[487]

★ Regime Change ★

The military might we enjoy becomes the "backing" of our currency. There are no other countries that can challenge our military superiority, and therefore they have little choice but to accept the dollars we declare are today's "gold." This is why countries that challenge the system–like Iraq, Iran, and Venezuela–become targets of our plans for regime change.[488]

Regime-change plans—whether by CIA operations or by preemptive war—almost always go badly. American involvement in installing the Shah of Iran in the 1950s, killing Diem in South Vietnam in the 1960s, helping Osama bin Laden against the Soviets in the 1980s, assisting Saddam Hussein against Iran in the 1980s, propping up dictators in many Arab countries, and supporting the destruction of the Palestinian people all have had serious repercussions on American interests including the loss of American life. We have wasted hundreds of billions of dollars while the old wounds in the Middle East continue to fester.[489]

Is a policy that replaces a bad regime with a worse regime the wisest course to follow?[490]

"Regime change" was supposed to mean that once Saddam Hussein was overthrown, the Iraqi people would run their own affairs.[491]

★ Republic ★

At the close of the Constitutional Convention in Philadelphia on September 18, 1787, a Mrs. Powel anxiously awaited the results, and as

Benjamin Franklin emerged from the long task now finished, asked him directly: "Well, Doctor, what have we got, a republic or a monarchy?" "A republic, if you can keep it," responded Franklin.[492]

The blessings of liberty resulting from the republic our forefathers designed have far surpassed the wildest dreams of all previous generations.[493]

It meant a lot more than just representative government and was a form of government in stark contrast to pure democracy where the majority dictated laws and rights.[494]

★ Roe vs. Wade ★

The 1973 Roe vs. Wade ruling caused great harm in two distinct ways. First, it legalized abortion at any stage, establishing clearly that the Supreme

Court and the government condoned the cheapening of human life. Second, it firmly placed this crucial issue in the hands of the federal courts and national government. The federalization of abortion was endorsed even by those who opposed abortion. Instead of looking for state-by-state solutions and limiting federal court jurisdiction, those anxious to protect life came to rely on federal laws, eroding the Constitutional process.[495]

Decaying social and moral attitudes decades ago set the stage for the accommodated Roe vs. Wade ruling that nationalizes all laws dealing with abortion. The fallacious privacy argument the Supreme Court used must some day be exposed for the fraud that it is.[496]

The Supreme Court did not usher in the 1960s revolution that undermined the respect for all human life and liberty. Instead, the people's atti-

tude of the 1960s led to the Supreme Court Roe vs. Wade ruling in 1973 and contributed to a steady erosion of personal liberty.[497]

Getting a new Supreme Court that will overthrow Roe vs. Wade is a long shot despite the promises. **Remember, we already have a Supreme Court where seven of the nine members were appointed by Republican presidents with little to show for it.**[498]

Ron Paul 2008 Campaign

I'd like to think that I've introduced a brand-new idea into this campaign. I've even suggested that we follow the Constitution.[499]

I've sort of been able to gain credibility through the back door here, you know, running as a Republican and all of a sudden getting a lot of support, a lot of volunteers and a lot of money. It's getting pretty hard to be ignored.[500]

I don't want to be president for what I want to do; it's for what I don't want to do. I don't want to run the economy, I don't want to police the world. I don't want to tell people how to run their lives and spend their money.[501]

Every single day our numbers are growing exponentially, financially as well as volunteers. Our job is to get them to the polls, and it looks like we're moving in that direction. Everybody's pretty excited.[502]

So in many ways the campaign has found me as much as I have found them. It's not a top-down organization. It's sort of bottom-up.[503]

★

★ Ron Paul Revolution ★

It looks, indeed, like the revolution is spreading. And it looks like it will not be stopped.[504]

★

★ Ronald Reagan ★

We should heed the words of Ronald Reagan about his experience with a needless and mistaken military occupation of Lebanon. Sending troops into Lebanon seemed like a good idea in 1983, but in 1990 President Reagan said this in his memoirs: "We did not appreciate fully enough the depth of the hatred and complexity of the problems that made the Middle East

such a jungle. . . . In the weeks immediately after the bombing, I believed the last thing we should do was turn tail and leave . . . yet, the irrationality of Middle Eastern politics forced us to rethink our policy there."[505]

Ronald Reagan in 1983 sent Marines into Lebanon. And he said he would never turn tail and run. A few months later the Marines were killled. Two hundred and forty-one were killed, and the Marines were taken out. . . and he changed his policy there. **We need the courage of a Ronald Reagan.**[506]

★ Rule of Law ★

Some may argue that it does not matter whether the United States operates under double standards. We are the lone superpower and can do as we wish, they argue. But this is a problem of the rule of law. Are we a nation that respects the rule of law? **What example does it set for the rest of the world—including rising powers like China and Russia—when we change the rules of the game whenever we see fit? Won't this come back to haunt us?**[507]

All we have to do is obey the law. We were given great guidance coming out of the great city of Philadelphia on what we ought to be doing, and **we ought to just live up to our ideals.**[508]

★

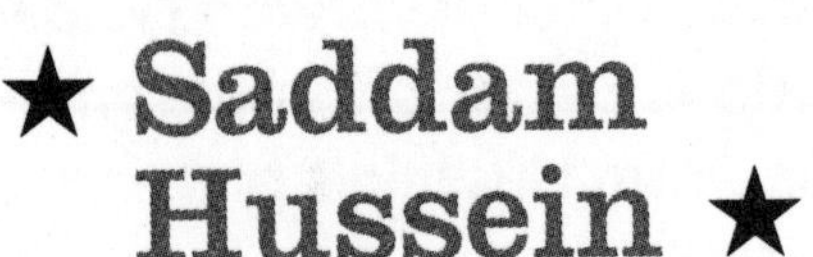

★ Saddam Hussein ★

Yes, Saddam Hussein is dead, and only the Sunnis mourn. The Shiites and Kurds celebrate his death, as do the Iranians and especially bin Laden—all enemies of Saddam Hussein. We have performed a tremendous service for both bin Laden

and Ahmadinejad, and it will cost us plenty. The violent reaction to our complicity in the execution of Saddam Hussein is yet to come.[509]

The final rhetorical refuge for those who defend the war, not yet refuted, is the dismissive statement that "the world is better off without Saddam Hussein." It implies no one can question anything we have done because of this fact. Instead of an automatic concession, it should be legitimate, though politically incorrect, to challenge this disarming assumption. **No one has to like or defend Saddam Hussein to point out we won't know whether the world is better off until someone has taken Saddam Hussein's place.**[510]

Why do we still not know who forged the documents claiming Saddam Hussein was about to buy uranium from Niger?[511]

The desire by American policy makers to engineer regime change in Iraq had been smoldering since the first Persian Gulf conflict in 1991. This reflected a dramatic shift in our policy, since in the 1980s we maintained a friendly alliance with Saddam Hussein as we assisted him in his war against our arch nemesis, the Iranian ayatollah. Most Americans ignore that we provided assistance to this ruthless dictator with biological and chemical weapons technology. We heard no complaints in the 1980s about his treatment of the Kurds and Shiites, or the ruthless war he waged against Iran. Our policy toward Iraq played a major role in convincing Saddam Hussein he had free rein in the Middle East, and the results demonstrate the serious shortcomings of our foreign policy of interventionism that we have followed now for over a hundred years.[512]

★ Sanctions ★

Proponents of such methods fail to remember that where goods cannot cross borders, troops will. Sanctions against Cuba, Iraq, and numerous other countries failed to topple their governments. Rather than weakening dictators, these sanctions strengthened their hold on power and led to more suffering on the part of the Cuban and Iraqi people. To the extent that divestment effected change in South Africa, it was brought about by private individuals working through the market to influence others.[513]

★

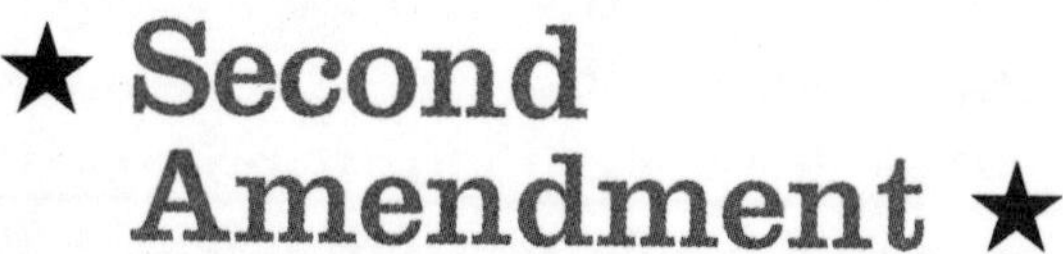

★ Second Amendment ★

Mr. Speaker, I rise to restore the right the founding fathers saw as the guarantee of every other right by introducing the Second Amendment Protection Act. This legislation reverses the steady erosion of the right to keep and bear arms by repealing unconstitutional laws that allow power-hungry federal bureaucrats to restrict the rights of law-abiding gun owners.[514]

Finally, my bill amends the Gun Control Act of 1968 by deleting the "sporting purposes" test, which allows the treasury secretary to infringe on Second Amendment rights by classifying a firearm (handgun, rifle, shotgun) as a "destructive device" simply because the secretary believes the gun to be "nonsporting."[515]

Thomas Jefferson said, "The constitutions of most of our States assert that all power is inherent in the people; . . . that it is their right and duty to be at all times armed." Jefferson, and all of the founders, would be horrified by the proliferation of unconstitutional legislation that prevents law-abiding Americans from exercising their right and duty to keep and bear arms. I hope my colleagues will join me in upholding the founders' vision for a free society by cosponsoring the Second Amendment Restoration Act.[516]

The Second Amendment is not about hunting deer or keeping a pistol in your nightstand. It is not about protecting oneself against common criminals. It is about preventing tyranny.[517]

It is practical, rather than alarmist, to understand that unarmed citizens cannot be secure in their freedoms. **It's convenient for gun banners to dismiss this argument by saying "That could never happen here; this is America"—but history shows that only vigilant people can keep government under control.[518]**

By banning certain weapons today, we may plant the seeds for tyranny to flourish ten, thirty, or fifty years from now.[519]

Tortured interpretations of the Second Amendment cannot change the fact that both the letter of the amendment itself and the legislative history conclusively show that the founders intended ordinary citizens to be armed.[520]

The notion that the Second Amendment confers rights only upon organized state-run militias is preposterous; the amendment is meaningless unless it protects the gun rights of individuals.[521]

Freedom does not preclude security.[522]

This, for me, is not a reactive position coming out of 9/11, but rather is an argument I've made for decades, claiming that meddling in the affairs of others is dangerous to our security and actually reduces our ability to defend ourselves.[523]

There is no need for us to be forced to choose between security and freedom.[524]

Giving up freedom does not provide greater security.[525]

Removing the power of the executive branch to wage war, as was done through our revolution and the writing of the Constitution, is now being casually sacrificed on the altar of security.[526]

We all can agree that aggression should be met with force and that providing national security is an ominous responsibility that falls on Congress' shoulders. **But avoiding useless and unjustifiable wars that threaten our whole system of government and security seems to be the more prudent thing to do.**[527]

There is no evidence, however, that government bureaucracy and huge funding can solve our nation's problems. The likelihood is that the unintended consequences of this new proposal will diminish our freedoms and do nothing to enhance our security.[528]

I have, for more than two decades, been severely critical of our post-World War II foreign policy. I have perceived it to be not in our best interest and have believed that it presented a serious danger to our security.[529]

★ September 11 ★

They came over here because we were over there. We occupy their territory. It would be like if the Chinese had their navy in the Gulf of Mexico.[550]

Absent our foreign occupations and support for certain governments in the Middle East and central Asia over the past fifty years, the 9/11 attack would have been far less likely to happen.[531]

They don't come here to attack us because we're rich and we're free. **They come and they attack us because we're over there.[532]**

★ Social Security ★

That is why I was heartened when recently, the

independent, nonpartisan National Taxpayers Union Foundation praised me as one of only seven members of the House of Representatives who voted not to spend one penny of the Social Security trust fund on other government programs last year. Right now nearly every politician is claiming to have saved Social Security, but according to this independent group, only seven members of Congress actually voted that way last year. Yes, this is exactly why I can sometimes vote with only a handful of others, because I pledged to not spend Social Security trust fund dollars on other programs. While many people in Washington say they agree; this nonpartisan organization says only a handful really vote that way.[533]

I believe that no funds should be spent out of the Social Security trust fund except to pay pensions to beneficiaries.[534]

Each year the president and Congress take the money Americans pay into Social Security and use it for purposes other than paying pensions. **Simply, they are stealing from our senior citizens.**[535]

The Social Security Preservation Act will restore Americans' faith in their retirement. It should be illegal for the government to use the trust fund for any purpose except administering the Social Security system.[536]

★ Sound Money ★

For at least four generations our government-run universities have systematically preached a monetary doctrine justifying the so-called wisdom of paper money over the "foolishness" of sound money. Not only that, paper money has worked surprisingly well in the past thirty-five years—the years the world has accepted pure paper money as currency.[537]

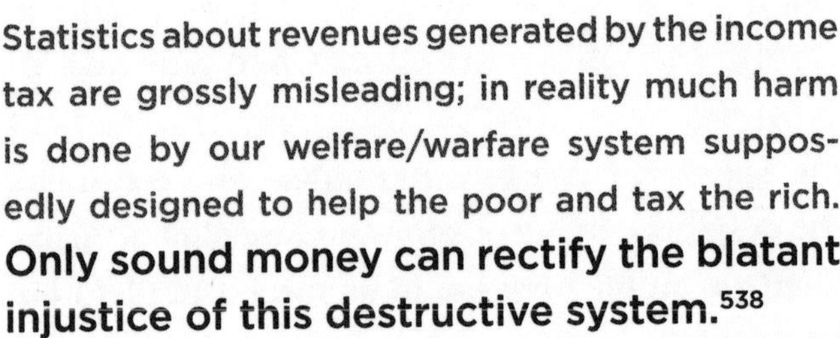

Statistics about revenues generated by the income tax are grossly misleading; in reality much harm is done by our welfare/warfare system supposedly designed to help the poor and tax the rich. **Only sound money can rectify the blatant injustice of this destructive system.**[538]

If one endorses small government and maximum liberty, one must support commodity money.[539]

Deficit financing by government is severely restricted by sound money.[540]

★ Space ★

Private enterprise depends on results and success and therefore private capital is always targeted much more wisely than are monies confiscated by governments.[541]

Mr. Speaker, I rise to congratulate and commend the designers, builders, sponsors, and pilot of SpaceShipOne on the occasion of its successful flight out of Earth's atmosphere on June 21, 2004. What is most remarkable about SpaceShipOne, of course, is that it is the first privately financed and privately built vehicle to leave Earth's atmosphere.[542]

SpaceShipOne was designed and built by Burt Rutan and piloted by test pilot Michael W. Melvill. It was launched successfully from Mojave, California, reaching a height of 100 Km (62 miles) above Earth's surface. Remarkably, SpaceShipOne is entirely privately financed, chiefly by Microsoft cofounder Paul G. Allen.[543]

According to the designers and financers of SpaceShipOne, the mission of this project is to demonstrate the viability of commercial space flight and to open the door for private space tourism. **The successful completion of SpaceShipOne's maiden voyage demonstrates that relatively modest amounts of private funding can significantly increase the boundaries of commercial space technology.**[544]

If only the United States had a taxation policy that limited government and thereby freed up more private capital, there is no telling how many more like Burt Rutan, Paul Allen, and Michael Melvill would be able to do great things to the benefit all of mankind.[545]

★

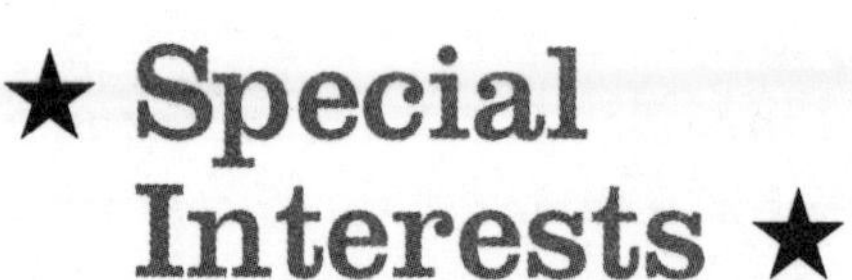

★ Special Interests ★

On top of this, the daily operation of Congress

reflects the power of special interests, not the will of the people–regardless of which party is in power.[546]

Special interests and the demented philosophy of conquest have driven most wars throughout history. Rarely has the cause of liberty, as it was in our own revolution, been the driving force. In recent decades our policies have been driven by neoconservative empire radicalism, profiteering in the military-industrial complex, misplaced do-good internationalism, mercantilistic notions regarding the need to control natural resources, and blind loyalty to various governments in the Middle East.[547]

As current policy further erodes the budget, special interests and members of Congress become even more aggressive in their efforts to capture a piece of the dwindling economic pie. That suc-

cess is the measure of effectiveness that guarantees a member's reelection.[548]

★

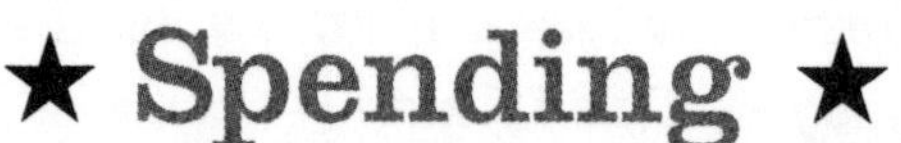

★ Spending ★

Whether it's war or welfare payments, it always means higher taxes, inflation, and debt.[549]

Huge omnibus spending bills, introduced at the end of the legislative year, are passed without scrutiny. No one individual knows exactly what is in the bill.[550]

Our spending habits, in combination with our flawed monetary system, if not changed will bring us a financial whirlwind that will make Katrina look like a minor storm.[551]

If Congress does not show some sense of financial restraint soon, we can expect the poor to become poorer; the middle class to become smaller; and the government to get bigger and more authoritarian—while the liberty of the people is diminished. **The illusion that deficits, printing money, and expanding the welfare and warfare states serves the people must come to an end.**[552]

It is now acceptable policy to spend excessively without worrying about debt limits.[553]

Congress has become like the drunk who promises to sober up tomorrow, if only he can keep drinking today. Does anyone really believe this will be the last time, that Congress will tighten its belt if we just grant it one last loan? What a joke! **There is only one approach to dealing with an incorrigible spendthrift: cut him off.**[554]

The problem is very simple: Congress almost always spends more each year than the IRS collects in revenues. Federal spending always goes up, but revenues are not so dependable, especially since raising income taxes to sufficiently fund the government would be highly unpopular. So long as Congress spends more than the government takes via taxes, the federal government must raise taxes, print more dollars, or borrow money.[555]

It is time Congress forces the federal government to live within its Constitutional means. **Congress should end the immoral practice of excessive spending and passing the bill to the next generation.**[556]

All spending ultimately must be a tax, even when direct taxes and direct borrowing are avoided.[557]

Every problem Congress and the administration create requires more money to fix. The mantra remains the same: Spend more money we don't have, borrow from the Chinese, or just print it.[558]

★ States' Rights ★

Many of my colleagues base their votes on issues regarding federalism on whether or not they agree with the particular state policy at issue. However, under the federalist system as protected by the Tenth Amendment to the United States Constitution, **states have the authority to legislate in ways that most members of Congress, and even the majority of the citizens of other states, disapprove.**[559]

Consistently upholding state autonomy does not mean approving of all actions taken by state governments; it simply means acknowledging that the Constitutional limits on federal power require Congress to respect the wishes of the states even when the states act unwisely.[560]

I would remind my colleagues that an unwise state law, by definition, only affects the people of one state. Therefore, it does far less damage than a national law that affects all Americans.[561]

★

★ Statism ★

Statism depends on the idea that the government owns us and citizens must obey. Confiscating the fruits of our labor through the income tax is crucial to the health of the state. The draft, or even the mere existence of the Selective Service, emphasizes that we will march off to war at the state's pleasure. A free society rejects all notions of involuntary servitude whether by draft or the confiscation of the fruits of our labor through the personal income tax.[562]

Many of the new laws passed after 9/11 had in fact been proposed long before that attack. The political atmosphere after that attack simply made it more possible to pass such legislation. The fear generated by 9/11 became an opportunity for those seeking to promote the power of the state domestically, just as it served to falsely justify the long planned-for invasion of Iraq.[563]

We can reclaim our heritage of freedom, not with a gun but with our voice. We can reject the creep of statism and encourage the blessings of liberty for our land. It will require work, and it will require commitment, and it will require a willingness to stand firm for our beliefs, refusing to compromise with those who would continue to push for more taxes, more spending, and more government solutions.[564]

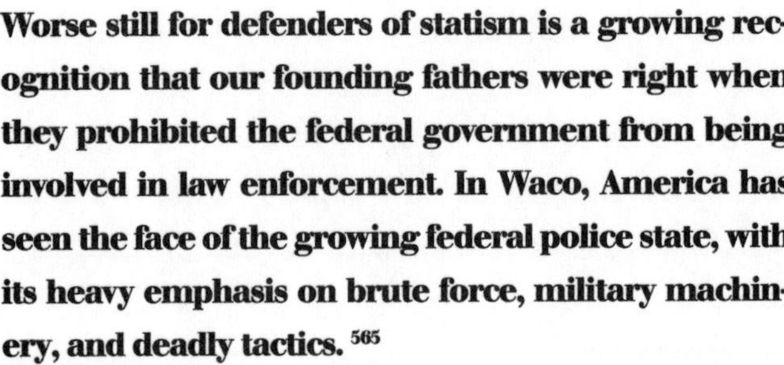

Worse still for defenders of statism is a growing recognition that our founding fathers were right when they prohibited the federal government from being involved in law enforcement. In Waco, America has seen the face of the growing federal police state, with its heavy emphasis on brute force, military machinery, and deadly tactics. [565]

★ Subsidies ★

The real problems arise when government planners give subsidies to energy companies and favor one form of energy over another.[566]

★ Sudan ★

We must realize the implications of urging the president to commit the United States to intervene in an ongoing civil war in a foreign land thousands of miles away.[567]

Can anyone tell me how sending thousands of American soldiers into harm's way in Sudan is by any stretch of the imagination in the U.S. national interest or in keeping with the Constitutional function of this country's military forces?[568]

How self-righteous a government is ours, which legally prohibits foreign campaign contributions (again with no Constitutional authority to regulate campaigns) yet assumes it knows best and, hence, supports dissident and insurgent groups in places like Cuba, Sudan, and around the world.[569]

It appears that this Congress has found a new mission for the Securities and Exchange Commission who are now tasked with investigating "the nature and extent of . . . commercial activity in Sudan" as it relates to "any violations of religious freedom and human rights in Sudan." It seems we have finally found a way to spend those excessive fees the SEC has been collecting from mutual fund investors (read: retirees) despite the fact we cannot seem to bring to the floor a bill to actually reduce those fees that have been collected in multiples above what is necessary to fund this agency's previous (and again unconstitutional) mission.[570]

★

★ Superpower ★

There is a pressing need to reassess our now widely accepted role as the world's lone superpower. If we don't, we are destined to reduce our nation to something far less powerful. [571]

★

★ Surveillance ★

It is argued that without government surveillance of every American, even without search warrants, security cannot be achieved. The sacrifice of some

liberty is required for security of our citizens, they claim.[572]

The administration assures us that domestic surveillance is done to protect us. But the crucial point is this: **Government assurances are not good enough in a free society. The overwhelming burden must always be placed on government to justify any new encroachment on our liberty.**[573]

It was once commonly held that an external force was the greatest threat to the liberty of American citizens. **Reality has proven that the greatest threat comes from within, and nowhere is this more apparent than in the growing surveillance state.**[574]

Some may claim that the federal government needs expanded surveillance powers to protect against fraud or some other criminal activities. However, monitoring the transactions of every American in order to catch those few who are involved in some sort of illegal activity turns one of the great bulwarks of our liberty, the presumption of innocence, on its head. **The federal government has no right to treat all Americans as criminals by spying on their relationship with their doctors, employers, or bankers.**[575]

★

★ Syria ★

We have been warned. Prepare for a broader war in the Middle East, as plans are being laid for the next U.S.-led regime change—in Syria. A UN report on the death of Lebanese Prime Minister Rafig Hariri elicited this comment from a senior U.S. policy maker: "Out of tragedy comes an extraordinary strategic opportunity." This statement reflects the continued neoconservative, Machiavellian influence on our foreign policy. The "opportunity" refers to the long-held neoconservative

plan for regime change in Syria, similar to what was carried out in Iraq.[576]

Syria already has been charged with developing weapons of mass destruction based on no more evidence than was available when Iraq was similarly charged.[577]

Syria has been condemned for not securing its borders, by the same U.S. leaders who cannot secure our own borders. Syria was castigated for placing its troops in Lebanon, a neighboring country, although such action was invited by an elected government and encouraged by the United States. The Syrian occupation of Lebanon elicited no suicide terrorist attacks, as was suffered by Western occupiers.[578]

Secretary Rice likewise sees the problems in Syria—that we helped to create—as an opportunity to advance our Middle Eastern agenda. In recent

testimony she stated that it was always the administration's intent to redesign the greater Middle East, and Iraq was only one part of that plan. And once again we have been told that all options are still on the table for dealing with Syria—including war.[579]

The statement that should scare all Americans (and the world) is the assurance by Secretary Rice that the president needs no additional authority from Congress to attack Syria. She argues that authority already has been granted by the resolutions on 9/11 and Iraq. This is not true, but if Congress remains passive to the powers assumed by the executive branch, it won't matter. As the war spreads, the only role for Congress will be to provide funding lest they be criticized for not supporting the troops. In the meantime, the Constitution and our liberties here at home will be further eroded as more Americans die.[580]

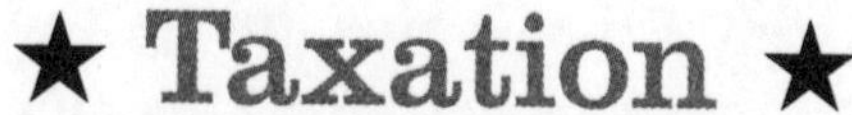

★ Taxation ★

Nearly everyone endorses exorbitant taxation; the only debate is about who should pay—either tax the producers and the rich or tax the workers and the poor through inflation and outsourcing jobs.[581]

A casual acceptance of the principle behind high taxation, with an income tax and an inheritance tax, is incompatible with a principled belief in a true republic. It is impossible to maintain a high tax system without the sacrifice of liberty and an undermining of property ownership. If kept in place, such a system will undermine prosperity, regardless of how well off we may presently be.[582]

I lean towards a flat tax, but I want to make it real flat like zero.[583]

★ The Left ★

It's important to recall that the left, in 2003, offered little opposition to the preemptive war in Iraq, and many are now not willing to stop it by defunding it or work to prevent an attack on Iran.[584]

★

★ Third Party Run ★

We're overseas spreading the message of democracy, but here if you're in a third party, you have a tough time. You can't get on ballots; you spend all of your time getting on ballots. You have to be a Ross Perot to even get on ballots. **The two parties are very much in control of the system, and they exclude individuals who aren't in that mold.**[585]

I've tried it before, and the laws are all so biased against third parties, that it is not on my agenda.[586]

★ Trade ★

I will also pursue true free trade with low tariffs and less burdensome regulation. However, I reject the "managed trade" approach of the World Trade Organization, North American Free Trade Agreement, and Central American Free Trade Agreement.[587]

It is known that countries that trade with each other and depend on each other for certain products and where the trade has been free and open and communications are free and open and travel is free and open, they are very less likely to fight wars.[588]

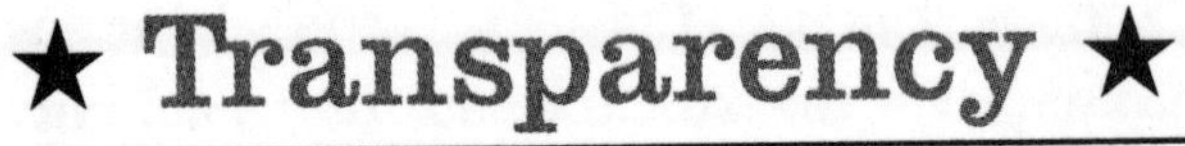

★ Transparency ★

When government spends the people's money, it must be done with utmost possible transparency.[589]

Transparency in monetary policy is a goal we should all support. I've often wondered why Congress so willingly has given up its prerogative over monetary policy. Astonishingly, Congress in essence has ceded total control over the value of our money to a secretive central bank.[590]

All meetings and decisions and actions by the President's Working Group on Financial Markets must be fully open to public scrutiny. If our government is artificially propping up the dollar by directly manipulating gold prices, or colluding with other central banks, it is information that belongs in the public domain. The same is true about any interference in the stock, bond, or commodity markets. **A free-market economy requires that government keeps its hands off and allows the consumers to exert their rightful control over the economy.**[591]

Congress, and especially the Financial Services Committee, must insist on total transparency and accuracy of all government financial statistics. **Any market interference by government agencies must be done in full public view.**[592]

★ Troop Withdrawal ★

I have been one of the strongest opponents of military action against Iraq. I voted against the initial authorization in 2002, and I have voted against every supplemental appropriations bill to

fund the war. I even voted against the initial "Iraq regime-change" legislation back in 1998. I believe our troops should be brought back to the United States without delay. Unfortunately, one of the reasons I oppose this legislation is that it masquerades as a troop withdrawal measure but in reality may well end up increasing U.S. commitments in the Middle East.[593]

Clearly the American public is overwhelmingly in favor of a withdrawal from Iraq, but Congress is not listening.[594]

Incoming congressional leaders have publicly stated their support for increasing troop levels, and Democrats have no intention of pursuing any serious withdrawal plan in Congress.[595]

★ United Nations ★

As my colleagues are well aware, I am strongly

opposed to the United Nations (UN) and our participation in that organization. Every Congress, I introduce a bill to get us out of the UN. But I also recognize problems with our demanding to have it both ways. On one hand, we pretend to abide by the UN and international law, such as when Congress cited the UN in its resolution authorizing the president to initiate war with Iraq. On the other hand, we feel free to completely ignore the terms of treaties—and even unilaterally demand a change in the terms of treaties—without hesitation. **This leads to an increasing perception around the world that we are no longer an honest broker, that we are not to be trusted. Is this the message we really want to send at this critical time?**[596]

Having already initiated a disastrous war against Iraq citing UN resolutions as justification, this resolution is like déja vu. Have we forgotten 2003 already? Do we really want to go to war again for UN resolutions? That is where this resolution, and the many others we have passed over the last sev-

eral years on Iran, is leading us. I hope my colleagues understand that a vote for this bill is a vote to move us closer to war with Iran.[597]

The UN once limited itself to disputes between nations; yet now it's assumed the UN, like the United States, has a legal and moral right to inject itself into the internal policies of sovereign nations. Yet what is the source of this presumed wisdom? Where is the moral imperative that allows us to become the judge and jury of a domestic murder in a country 6,000 miles from our shores?[598]

★

★ USSR ★

We contained the USSR and her thousands of nuclear warheads without military confrontation, leading to the collapse and disintegration of a powerful Soviet empire. Today we trade with Russia and her neighbors, as the market economy

spreads throughout the world without the use of arms.[599]

We must remember the Soviet system was not destroyed from without by military confrontation; it succumbed to the laws of economics that dictated communism a failure, and it was unable to finance its empire. **Deficit-financed welfarism, corporatism, Keynesianism, inflationism, and empire, American style, are no more economically sound than the more authoritarian approach of the Soviets.** If one is concerned with the red/blue division in this country and the strong feelings that exist already, an economic crisis will make the conflict much more intense.[600]

President Kennedy held firm and stood up to the Soviets as he should have and the confrontation was resolved. **What was not known at the time was the reassessment of**

our policy that placed nuclear missiles in the Soviets' backyard, in Turkey. These missiles were quietly removed a few months later, and the world became a safer place in which to live. Eventually, we won the Cold War without starting World War III.[601]

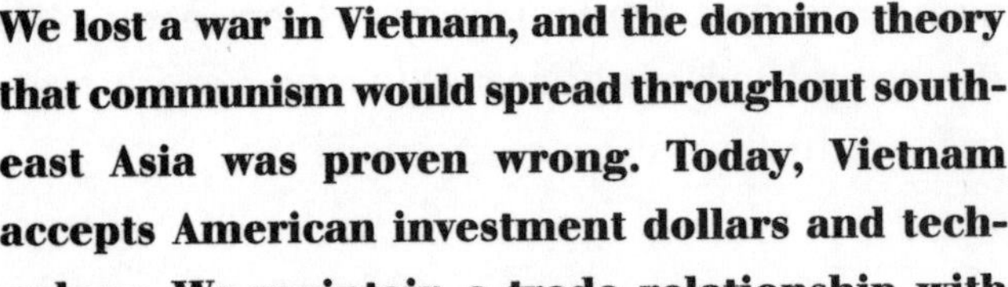

★ Vietnam ★

We lost a war in Vietnam, and the domino theory that communism would spread throughout southeast Asia was proven wrong. Today, Vietnam accepts American investment dollars and technology. We maintain a trade relationship with Vietnam that the war never achieved.[602]

We should not forget that what we did not achieve by military force in Vietnam was essentially achieved with the peace that came from our military failure and withdrawal of our armed forces. Today, through trade and peace,

U.S. investment and economic cooperation [have] Westernized Vietnam far more than our military efforts.[603]

★

★ Vice Presidency ★

It would be real hard for me to accept a vice presidency in an administration that endorsed everything I didn't believe in. I wouldn't be able to do that, and right now there aren't too many on the Republican side who are advocating nonintervention overseas.[604]

★

★ War ★

I will never take this country to war without a declaration of war from Congress.[605]

★

One of the strongest restraints against unnecessary war is a gold standard.[606]

The public too often only smells the stench of war after the killing starts. Public objection comes later on, but eventually it helps to stop the war.[607]

Policy changes in wartime are difficult, for it is almost impossible for the administration to change course since so much emotional energy has been invested in the effort. That's why Eisenhower ended the Korean War, and not Truman. That's why Nixon ended the Vietnam War, and not LBJ. Even in the case of Vietnam, the end was too slow and costly, as more then 30,000 military deaths came after Nixon's election in 1968. It makes a lot more sense to avoid unnecessary wars than to overcome the politics involved in stopping them once started. I personally am convinced that many of our wars could be prevented by paying stricter attention to the method whereby our troops are committed to battle. I also am convinced that when Congress does not declare war, victory is unlikely.[608]

Wartime spending money is appropriated and attached to emergency relief funds, making it difficult for politicians to resist.[609]

The First World War was sold to the American people as the war to end all wars. Instead, history shows it was the war that caused the twentieth century to be the most war-torn century in history. Our entry into World War I helped lead us into World War II, the Cold War, the Korean War, and the Vietnam War. Even our current crisis in the Middle East can be traced to the great wars of the twentieth century. **Though tens of millions of deaths are associated with these wars, we haven't learned a thing.**[610]

Randolph Bourne said that "war is the health of the state." With war, he argued, the state thrives. Those who believe in the powerful state see war as an opportunity. Those who mistrust the

people and the market for solving problems have no trouble promoting a "war psychology" to justify the expansive role of the state.[611]

Economic interests almost always are major reasons for wars being fought. Noble and patriotic causes are easier to sell to a public who must pay and provide cannon fodder to defend the financial interests of a privileged class.[612]

War reflects the weakness of a civilization that refuses to offer peace as an alternative.[613]

It seems that the people and Congress are easily persuaded by the jingoism of the preemptive war promoters. **It's only after the cost in human life and dollars are tallied up that the people object to unwise militarism.**[614]

In this war, like all others, the propagandists and promoters themselves don't fight, nor do their children. It's always worth the effort to wage war when others must suffer and die. Many of those who today pump the nation up with war fever were nowhere to be found when their numbers were called in the 1960s—when previous presidents and Congresses thought so little about sending young men off to war. Then it was in their best interests to find more important things to do—despite the so-called equalizing draft.[615]

A defensive war is morally permissible and justified, even required.[616]

Economic hardship is great in all wars. War is never economically beneficial except for those in posi-

tion to profit from war expenditures. The great tragedy of war is that it enables the careless disregard for civil liberties of our own people. Abuses of German and Japanese Americans in World War I and World War II are well-known.[617]

★ War Mentality ★

The war mentality was generated by the Iraq war in combination with the constant drumbeat of fear at home. Al-Qaeda and Osama bin Laden, who is now likely residing in Pakistan, our supposed ally, are ignored, as our troops fight and die in Iraq and are made easier targets for the terrorists in their backyard. **While our leaders constantly use the mess we created to further justify the erosion of our Constitutional rights here at home, we forget about our own borders and support the inexorable move toward global government—hardly a good plan for America.[618]**

★ War on Drugs ★

Applying to doctors laws intended to deal with drug kingpins, the government has created the illusion of some success in the war on drugs. Investigating drug dealers can be hard and dangerous work. In comparison, it is much easier to shut down medical practices and prosecute doctors who prescribe pain medication.[619]

A doctor who is willing to treat chronic pain patients with medically justified amounts of controlled substances may appear at first look to be excessively prescribing. Because so few doctors are willing to take the drug war prosecution risks associated with treating chronic pain patients, and because chronic pain patients must often consume significant doses of pain medication to obtain relief, the prosecution of one pain doctor can be heralded as a large success. All the government needs to do is point to the large

amount of patients and drugs associated with a medical practice.[620]

Our prisons overflow, with the cost of enforcement now into the hundreds of billions of dollars, yet drug use is not reduced.[621]

Our prisons are flooded with nonviolent drug users—84 percent of all federal prisoners—but no serious reassessment is considered.[622]

★

★ War on Terrorism ★

We are constantly told that the next terrorist attack could come at any moment. Rather than questioning why we might be attacked, this atmosphere of fear instead prompts giving up liberty and privacy. 9/11 has been conveniently used

to generate the fear necessary to expand both our foreign intervention and domestic surveillance.[623]

Declaring war against Islamic fascism or terrorism is vague and meaningless. This enemy we're fighting at the expense of our own liberties is purposely indefinable. Therefore the government will exercise wartime powers indefinitely. We've been fully warned to expect a long, long war.[624]

The catch-all phrase, "War on Terrorism," in all honesty, has no more meaning than if one wants to wage a war against criminal gangsterism. **It's deliberately vague and nondefinable to justify and permit perpetual war anywhere, and under any circumstances.** Don't forget: The Iraqis and Saddam Hussein had absolutely nothing to do with any terrorist attack against us including that on 9/11.[625]

Whenever a war is ongoing, civil liberties are under attack at home. The current war in Iraq and the misnamed war on terror have created an environment here at home that affords little Constitutional protection of our citizen's rights. Extreme nationalism is common during wars. Signs of this are now apparent.[626]

Immediately after the attack on September 11, 2001, I introduced several pieces of legislation designed to help fight terrorism and secure the United States, including a bill to allow airline pilots to carry firearms and a bill that would have expedited the hiring of Federal Bureau of Investigation (FBI) translators to support counterterrorism investigations and operations. I also introduced a bill to authorize the president to issue letters of marque and reprisal to bring to justice those who committed the attacks of September 11, 2001, and other similar acts of war planned for the future.[627]

Until we consider the root causes of terrorism, beyond the jingoistic explanations offered thus far, we will not defeat terrorism and we will not be safer.[628]

★ War Policy ★

The most important thing Congress can do to prevent needless and foolish wars is for every member to take seriously his or her oath to obey the Constitution. Wars should be entered into only after great deliberation and caution. Wars that are declared by Congress should reflect the support of the people, and the goal should be a quick and successful resolution.[629]

Our undeclared wars over the past sixty-five years have dragged on without precise victories. We fight to spread American values, to enforce UN resolutions, and to slay supposed Hitlers. We for-

get that we once spread American values by persuasion and setting an example—not by bombs and preemptive invasions. Nowhere in the Constitution are we permitted to go to war on behalf of the United Nations at the sacrifice of our national sovereignty. We repeatedly use military force against former allies, thugs we helped empower—like Saddam Hussein and Osama bin Laden—even when they pose no danger to us.[630]

★ War Profiteers ★

Who possibly benefits from escalating chaos in Iraq? **Neoconservatives unabashedly have written about how chaos presents opportunities for promoting their goals.** Certainly Osama bin Laden has benefited from the turmoil in Iraq, as have the Iranian Shiites who now are better positioned to take control of southern Iraq.[631]

Congress could not resist the opportunity to put its hands in taxpayers' pockets by adding 20 billion dollars in completely unrelated spending to the final bill. In essence, Congress is so addicted to spending that it will use any opportunity, even a war, to spend money for every conceivable reason—however unrelated to the war in Iraq.[632]

★ War Propaganda ★

Propaganda is pushed on our troops to exploit their need to believe in a cause that's worth the risk to life and limb.[633]

Proponents of the war do not hesitate to challenge the manhood of war critics, accusing them of wanting to cut and run. Some war supporters ducked military service themselves while others fought and died, only adding to the anger of those

who have seen battle up close and now question our campaign in Iraq.[634]

★

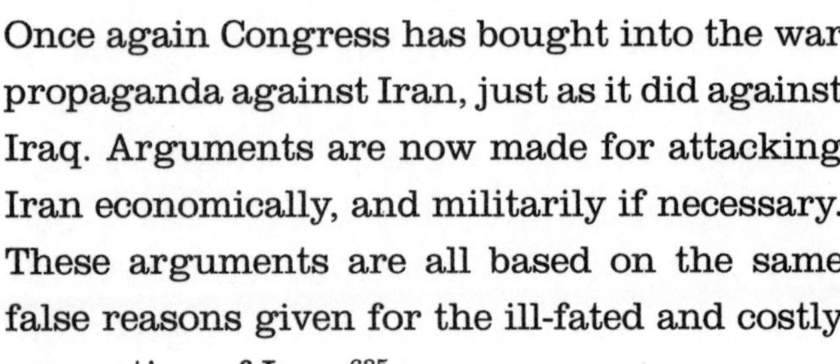

Once again Congress has bought into the war propaganda against Iran, just as it did against Iraq. Arguments are now made for attacking Iran economically, and militarily if necessary. These arguments are all based on the same false reasons given for the ill-fated and costly occupation of Iraq.[635]

★

The whipped-up war propaganda too often overrules the logic that should prevail.[636]

★

★ War Spending ★

The cost of war is enormously detrimental; it significantly contributes to the economic instability of the nation by boosting spending, deficits, and inflation. Funds used for war are funds that could have remained in the productive economy to raise the standard of living of Americans now unemployed, underemployed, or barely living on the margin. Yet even these costs may be preferable to paying for war with huge tax increases. This is because although fiat dollars are theoretically worthless, value is imbued by the trust placed in them by the world's financial community. **Subjective trust in a currency can override objective knowledge about government policies, but only for a limited time.**[637]

Much of the expense of the Persian Gulf War in 1991 was shouldered by many of our willing allies. That's not so today. Now, more than ever, the dollar hegemony—its dominance as the world reserve currency—is required to finance our huge war expenditures. This $2 trillion never-ending war must be paid for, one way or another. Dollar hegemony provides the vehicle to do just that.[638]

For the most part the true victims aren't aware of how they pay the bills. The license to create money out of thin air allows the bills to be paid through price inflation. American citizens, as well as average citizens of Japan, China, and other countries, suffer from price inflation, which represents the "tax" that pays the bills for our military adventures. That is until the fraud is discovered, and the foreign producers decide not to take dollars nor hold them very long in payment for their goods. Everything possible is done to prevent the fraud of the monetary system from being exposed to the masses who suffer from it. If oil markets replace dollars with Euros, it would in time curtail our ability to continue to print, without restraint, the world's reserve currency.[639]

We should not fight, because it's simply not worth it. What are we going to get for nearly 2,000 soldier deaths and twenty thousand severe casualties? Was the $350 billion worth it? This is a cost that will be passed on to future generations through an expanded national debt. I'll bet most Americans can think of a lot better ways to have spent this money. Today's program of guns and butter will be more damaging to our economy than a similar program was in the 1960s, which gave us the stagflation of the 1970s. **The economic imbalances today are much greater than they were in those decades.**[640]

★ Warfare ★

Short wars, with well-defined victories, are tolerated by the American people even when they are misled as to the reasons for the war. Wars entered into without a proper declaration tend to be politically motivated and not for national security reasons. These wars, by their very nature, are prolonged, costly, and usually require a new administration to finally end them. This certainly was true with the Korean and Vietnam Wars. The lack of a quick military success, the loss of life and limb, and the huge economic costs of lengthy wars precipitate anger. This is overwhelmingly true when the war propaganda that stirred up illegitimate fears is exposed as a fraud. Most soon come to realize the promise of guns and butter is an illusion. **They come to understand that inflation, a weak economy, and a prolonged war without real success are the reality.**[641]

★

★ Washington ★

At home I'm frequently asked about my frustration with Congress, since so many reform proposals go unheeded. I jokingly reply, "No, I'm never frustrated, because I have such low expectations." But the American people have higher expectations, and without forthcoming solutions, are beyond frustrated with their government.[642]

Nothing will change in Washington until it's recognized that the ultimate driving force behind most politicians is obtaining and holding power. And money from special interests drives the political process.

Money and power are important only because the government wields power not granted by the Constitution. A limited, Constitutional government would not tempt special interests to buy the politicians who wield power. The whole process feeds on itself. **Everyone is rewarded by ignoring Constitutional restraints while expanding and complicating the entire bureaucratic state.**[643]

★

★ Wealth ★

Few understand that our consumption and apparent wealth is dependent on a current account deficit of $800 billion per year. **This deficit shows that much of our prosperity is based on borrowing rather than a true increase in production.** Statistics show year after year that our productive manufacturing jobs continue to go overseas. This phenomenon is not seen as a consequence of the international fiat monetary system, where the United States government benefits as the issuer of the world's reserve currency.[644]

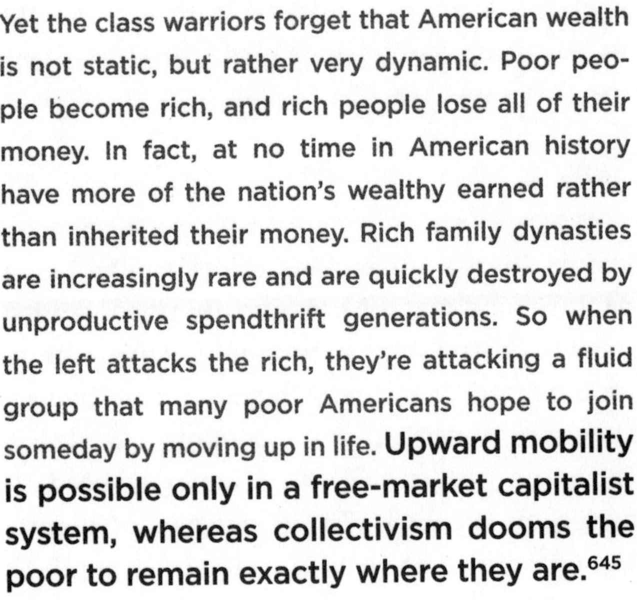

Yet the class warriors forget that American wealth is not static, but rather very dynamic. Poor people become rich, and rich people lose all of their money. In fact, at no time in American history have more of the nation's wealthy earned rather than inherited their money. Rich family dynasties are increasingly rare and are quickly destroyed by unproductive spendthrift generations. So when the left attacks the rich, they're attacking a fluid group that many poor Americans hope to join someday by moving up in life. **Upward mobility is possible only in a free-market capitalist system, whereas collectivism dooms the poor to remain exactly where they are.**[645]

★ Welfare ★

And the sad part is that the sincere efforts to help people do better economically through welfare programs always fail. Dependency replaces self-reliance while the sense of self-worth of the recipient suffers, making for an angry, unhappy, and

dissatisfied society. The cost in dollar terms is high, but the cost in terms of liberty is even greater, but generally ignored, and in the long run, there's nothing to show for this sacrifice.[646]

Today, there's no serious effort to challenge welfare as a way of life, and its uncontrolled growth in the next economic downturn is to be expected. Too many citizens now believe they are "entitled" to monetary assistance from the government anytime they need it, and they expect it. Even in times of plenty, the direction has been to continue expanding education, welfare, and retirement benefits. No one asks where the government gets the money to finance the welfare state. Is it morally right to do so? Is it authorized in the Constitution? Does it help anyone in the long run? Who suffers from the policy? **Until these questions are seriously asked and correctly answered, we cannot expect the march toward a pervasive welfare state to stop, and we can expect**

our liberties to be continuously compromised.[647]

The welfare state is unmanageable and severely overextended. In spite of hopes that supposed reform would restore sound financing and provide for all the needs of the people, it's becoming more apparent every day that the entire system of entitlements is in a precarious state and may well collapse.[648]

★

★ Wilsonian Idealism ★

Eventually, we will come to realize that the Wilsonian idealism of using America's resources to promote democracy around the world through force is a seriously flawed policy. Wilson pretended to be spreading democracy worldwide, and yet women in the United States at that time were not allowed to vote. Democracy, where the majority dictates

the rules, cannot protect minorities and individual rights. And in addition, using force to impose our will on others almost always backfires. There's no reason that our efforts in the twenty-first century to impose a Western-style government in Iraq will be any more successful than the British were after World War I. This especially can't work if democracy is only an excuse for our occupation and the real reasons are left unrecognized.[649]

Promoting democracy is now our nation's highest ideal. Wilson started it with his ill-advised drive to foolishly involve us in World War I. His utopian dream was to make the world safe for democracy. Instead, his naiveté and arrogance promoted our involvement in the back-to-back tragedies of World War I and World War II. It's hard to imagine the rise of Hitler in World War II without the Treaty of Versailles. But this has not prevented every president since Wilson from promoting U.S.-style democracy to the rest of the world.[650]

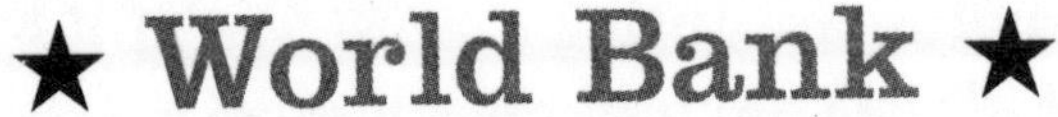

World Bank

Like many bureaucracies, the World Bank has constantly attempted to reinvent itself and redefine its mission. Some critics have referred to this as "mission creep." **It is the reaction of self-interested bureaucrats who are intent on saving their jobs at all costs.** The noninstitutional elements of Bretton Woods, such as the gold-backed dollar standard, have gone by the wayside, but the World Bank and the International Monetary Fund soldier on.[651]

What is most annoying about the World Bank is the criticisms alleging that the bank and its actions demonstrate the negative side of free-market capitalism. Nothing could be further from the truth. The World Bank is not an organization devoted to capitalism, or to the free market, but to state-run corporate capitalism. Established and managed by a multitude of national governments, the World Bank promotes managed trade, by which politically connected individuals

and corporations enrich themselves at the expense of the poor and middle class.[652]

Western governments tax their citizens to fund the World Bank, lend this money to corrupt third-world dictators who abscond with the funds and then demand repayment that is extracted through taxation from poor third-world citizens, rather than from the government officials responsible for the embezzlement. **It is in essence a global transfer of wealth from the poor to the rich.** Taxpayers around the world are forced to subsidize the lavish lifestyles of third-world dictators and highly paid World Bank bureaucrats who don't even pay income tax.[653]

The World Bank has outlived its intended purpose. Capital markets are flush with money and well developed enough to lend money not just to national governments but to local and regional development projects at competitive market rates. In the aftermath of Mr. Wolfowitz's departure, much will be made of the question of his successor, when **the questioning instead should be directed towards the phasing out of the organization.**[654]

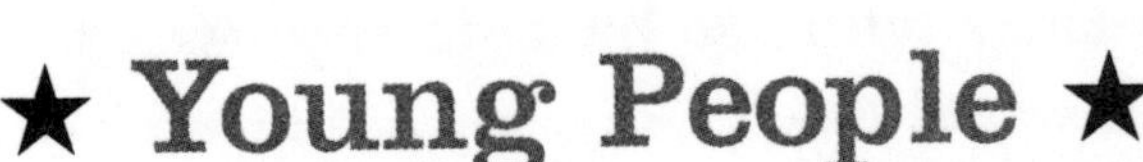

I make them feel good that you can be conservative and pro-truth and pro-American and pro-Constitution and not want to go to war for needless purposes. **They've been made to feel . . . that if you don't support all these invasions and all this fighting, somehow you're anti-American.**[655]

I continue to be amazed at how many young people are interested in our campaign and by how smart and informed they are. I think they come because they see what they are poised to inherit and they aren't happy. We are handing our children countless trillions of dollars of debt and mortgaging their future. If we don't do something, this will be the first American generation that lives more poorly than their parents. **Young people want to be free; they don't want the government running their lives; they want to be able to opt out of the entitlement system; and they want to be able to take care of themselves.**[656]

★

Notes

[1] Ron Paul, "Where to from Here?" U.S. House of Representatives, Nov. 20, 2004.

[2] Ibid.

[3] Ibid.

[4] Steven Colbert, Interview with Ron Paul, *The Colbert Report*, June 13, 2007.

[5] Liz Halloran, "Q&A: Presidential Candidate Ron Paul," *U.S. News & World Report*, Nov. 9, 2007.

[6] Ron Paul, "The Crucial Moral Issue: Respect for Life," U.S. House of Representatives, Nov. 20, 2004.

[7] Ibid.

[8] Ibid.

[9] Ron Paul, "Statement on the 'Sunlight Rule'," U.S. House of Representatives, March 3, 2006.

[10] Ibid.

[11] Ibid.

[12] Ibid.

[13] Ron Paul, "Making the World Safe for Christianity," U.S. House of Representatives, March 28, 2006.

[14] Ron Paul, "Keep Your Eye on the Target," U.S. House of Representatives, Nov. 29, 2001.

[15] Ron Paul, Speech, U.S. House of Representatives, Sept. 25, 2001.

[16] Ron Paul, "U.S. Taxpayers Send Billions to our Enemies in Afghanistan," *Texas Straight Talk*, Nov. 5, 2001.

[17] Ibid.

[18] Ron Paul, "Why We Should Not Fight," U.S. House of Representatives, Sept. 8, 2005.

[19] Ron Paul, "Questions That Won't Be asked about Iraq," U.S. House of Representatives, Sept. 10, 2002.

[20] Ibid.

[21] Ibid.

[22] Ibid.

[23] Ron Paul, "The Blame Game," U.S. House of Representatives, Dec. 7, 2005.

[24] Jarret Wollstein, "The Future of the Dollar, Entitlements, and the U.S. Economy," International Society for Individual Liberty, April 24, 2006.

[25] Ron Paul, "Statement on So-Called 'Deficit Reduction Act'," U.S. House of Representatives, Nov. 18, 2005.

[26] Ron Paul, "Pain at the Pump," *Texas Straight Talk*, 2007.

[27] Ron Paul, "End the Two-Party Monopoly!" U.S. House of Representatives, July 15, 2004.

[28] Ibid.

[29] Ibid.

[30] Ron Paul, "What the Price of Gold Is Telling Us," U.S. House of Representatives, April 25, 2006.

[31] Ron Paul, Speech, U.S. House of Representatives, June 13, 2007.

[32] Ron Paul, "A Flood of Bills of Rights," *Texas Straight Talk*, Aug. 16, 1999.

[33] Ibid.

[34] Ron Paul, "Big Government Solutions Don't Work," U.S. House of Representatives, Sept. 7, 2006.

[35] Ron Paul, "The Blame Game," U.S. House of Representatives, Dec. 7, 2005.

[36] Ibid.

[37] Ibid.

[38] Ron Paul, "Searching for a New Direction," U.S. House of Representatives, Jan. 18, 2006.

[39] Ron Paul, "Where to from Here?" U.S. House of Representatives, Nov. 20, 2004.

[40] Ron Paul, "Government Spending: A Tax on the Middle Class," U.S. House of Representatives, July 8, 2004.

[41] Ibid.

[42] Ibid.

[43] Ron Paul, "Statement on Introduction of the Congressional Responsibility and Accountability Act," U.S. House of Representatives, Aug. 1, 2007.

[44] Ibid.

[45] Ron Paul, Speech, U.S. House of Representatives, Aug. 1, 2007.

[46] Ron Paul, "A Republic, If You Can Keep It," U.S. House of Representatives, Jan. 31 and Feb. 2, 2000.

[47] Ron Paul, "House Financial Services Committee, Subcommittee on Domestic and International, Monetary Policy," U.S. House of Representatives, Oct. 17, 2007.

[48] Ron Paul, "None of Your Business!" *Texas Straight Talk*, July 12, 2004.

[49] Ron Paul, "Business as Usual in Washington?" *Texas Straight Talk*, Oct. 29, 2001.

[50] Ron Paul, "Repeal Sarbanes-Oxley!" U.S. House of Representatives, April 14, 2005.

[51] Ron Paul, "What the Price of Gold Is Telling Us," U.S. House of Representatives, April 25, 2006.

[52] Ibid.

[53] Ibid.

[54] Ron Paul, "The End of Dollar Hegemony," U.S. House of Representatives, Feb. 12, 2006.

[55] Ibid.

[56] Ron Paul, "Sorry, Mr. Franklin, We're All Democrats Now'," U.S. House of Representatives, Jan. 29, 2003.

[57] Ron Paul, "Iran: The Next Neocon Target," U.S. House of Representatives, April 5, 2006.

[58] Ibid.

[59] Ron Paul, "Searching for a New Direction," U.S. House of Representatives, Jan. 18, 2006.

[60] Ron Paul, "Congressman Paul's Statement in Opposition to HR 552," U.S. House of Representatives, Sept. 4, 2007.

[61] Ron Paul, "Staying or Leaving," U.S. House of Representatives, Oct. 7, 2005.

[62] "A New China Policy," U.S. House of Representatives, April 25, 2001.

[63] Ron Paul, "Making the World Safe for Christianity," U.S. House of Representatives, March 28, 2006.

[64] Ron Paul, "The Crucial Moral Issue: Respect for Life," U.S. House of Representatives, Nov. 20, 2004.

[65] Ron Paul, "The 9/11 Intelligence Bill: More Bureaucracy, More Intervention, Less Freedom," U.S. House of Representatives, Oct. 8, 2004.

[66] Judy Woodruff, "Paul Envisions Smaller Government, Less Global Intervention," PBS, Oct. 12, 2007.

[67] Ron Paul, Speech, U.S. House of Representatives, Sept. 25, 2001.

[68] Ibid.

[69] Ron Paul, "In the Name of Patriotism (Who Are the Patriots?)," U.S. House of Representatives, June 6, 2007.

[70] Ibid.

[71] Ron Paul, "Big Government Solutions Don't Work," U.S. House of Representatives, Sept. 7, 2006.

[72] Ron Paul, "In the Name of Patriotism (Who Are the Patriots?)," U.S. House of Representatives, June 6, 2007.

[73] Ibid.

[74] Ibid.

[75] Ibid.

[76] Ibid.

[77] Ron Paul, "The Blame Game," U.S. House of Representatives, Dec. 7, 2005.

[78] Ron Paul, "Searching for a New Direction," U.S. House of Representatives, Jan. 18, 2006.

[79] Ron Paul, "In Search of a Cause," *Texas Straight Talk*, Oct. 25, 1999.

[80] Ron Paul, "Statement on So-Called 'Deficit Reduction Act'," U.S. House of Representatives, Nov. 18, 2005.

[81] Ron Paul, "March (Budget) Madness," *Texas Straight Talk*, March 29, 2004.

[82] Ron Paul, "A Token Attempt to Reduce Government Spending," U.S. House of Representatives, June 24, 2004.

[83] Ron Paul, "Cultural Conservatives Lose If Gay Marriage Is Federalized," U.S. House of Representatives, Sept. 30, 2004.

[84] Ron Paul, "Neo Conned," U.S. House of Representatives, July 10, 2003.

[85] Ibid.

[86] Steven Colbert, Interview with Ron Paul, *The Colbert Report*, June 13, 2007.

[87] Ron Paul, "Statement on the Iraq War Resolution," U.S. House of Representatives, Feb. 14, 2007.

[88] Ron Paul, "The Scandal at Walter Reed," U.S. House of Representatives, March 7, 2007.

[89] Ron Paul, "The Blame Game," U.S. House of Representatives, Dec. 7, 2005.

[90] Ron Paul, "The Law of Opposites," U.S. House of Representatives, Sept. 7, 2006.

[91] Ron Paul, "Reconsidering the Patriot Act," *Texas Straight Talk,* May 2, 2005.

[92] Ron Paul, "Torture, War, and Presidential Powers," *Texas Straight Talk,* June 14, 2004.

[93] Ron Paul, "The Law of Opposites," U.S. House of Representatives, Sept. 7, 2006.

[94] Ibid.

[95] Ron Paul, "Federal Courts and the Pledge of Allegiance," U.S. House of Representatives, Sept. 23, 2004.

[96] Ibid.

[97] Ron Paul, "Protecting Marriage from Judicial Tyranny," U.S. House of Representatives, July 22, 2004.

[98] Ibid.

[99] Ibid.

[100] Ibid.

[101] Ibid.

[102] Ibid.

[103] Ron Paul, "Searching for a New Direction," U.S. House of Representatives, Jan. 18, 2006.

[104] Ron Paul, "Where to from Here?" U.S. House of Representatives, Nov. 20, 2004.

[105] Ron Paul, "Raising the Debt Limit: A Disgrace," U.S. House of Representatives, Nov. 18, 2004.

[106] Ibid.

[107] Ron Paul, "Iran: The Next Neocon Target," U.S. House of Representatives, April 5, 2006.

[108] Ron Paul, "The Blame Game," U.S. House of Representatives, Dec. 7, 2005.

[109] Ron Paul, "Why We Fight," U.S. House of Representatives, Sept. 8, 2005.

[110] Ibid.

[111] GOP Presidential Debate, Columbia, SC, *Fox News,* May 2007.

[112] Ron Paul, "Big Government Solutions Don't Work," U.S. House of Representatives, Sept. 7, 2006.

[113] Ibid.

[114] Ron Paul, "Where to from Here?" U.S. House of Representatives, Nov. 20, 2004.

[115] Ron Paul, "The Law of Opposites," U.S. House of Representatives, Sept. 7, 2006.

[116] Ron Paul, "Escalation Is Hardly the Answer," U.S. House of Representatives, Jan. 11, 2007.

[117] Ron Paul, "Making the World Safe for Christianity," U.S. House of Representatives, March 28, 2006.

[118] Ron Paul, "Why We Fight," U.S. House of Representatives, Sept. 8, 2005.

[119] Ron Paul, "The Republican Congress Wastes Billions Overseas," U.S. House of Representatives, July 20, 2005.

[120] Ibid.

[121] Ron Paul, "Searching for a New Direction," U.S. House of Representatives, Jan. 18, 2006.

[122] Ron Paul, "What the Price of Gold Is Telling Us," U.S. House of Representatives, April 25, 2006.

[123] Ibid.

[124] Ibid.

[125] Ibid.

[126] Ron Paul, "The End of Dollar Hegemony," U.S. House of Representatives, Feb. 12, 2006.

[127] Ron Paul, "Searching for a New Direction," U.S. House of Representatives, Jan. 18, 2006.

[128] Ibid.

[129] Ron Paul, "Iran: The Next Neocon Target," U.S. House of Representatives, April 5, 2006.

[130] Ron Paul, "The Law of Opposites," U.S. House of Representatives, Sept. 7, 2006.

[131] Ron Paul, "Iran: The Next Neocon Target," U.S. House of Representatives, April 5, 2006.

[132] Ron Paul, "3000 American Deaths in Iraq," U.S. House of Representatives, Jan. 5, 2007.

[133] Ibid.

[134] Ron Paul, "Reject Draft Slavery," U.S. House of Representatives, Oct. 5, 2004.

[135] Ibid.

[136] Ibid.

[137] Ibid.

[138] Ibid.

[139] Ibid.

[140] Ron Paul, "A Republic, If You Can Keep It," U.S. House of Representatives, Jan. 31 and Feb. 2, 2000.

[141] Ron Paul, "Why Are Americans So Angry?" U.S. House of Representatives, June 29, 2006.

[142] Ron Paul, "The Law of Opposites," U.S. House of Representatives, Sept. 7, 2006.

[143] Ibid.

[144] Ron Paul, "Opening Statement Committee on Financial Services, Paulson Hearing," U.S. House of Representatives, June 20, 2007.

[145] Ron Paul, "A Republic, If You Can Keep It," U.S. House of Representatives, Jan. 31 and Feb. 2, 2000.

[146] Ibid.

[147] Ron Paul, "Parents Must Have Control of Education," *Texas Straight Talk*, July 20, 1997.

[148] Ron Paul, "Statement on HR 609, the 'Academic Bill of Rights'," U.S. House of Representatives, March 29, 2006.

[149] Ron Paul, "Making the World Safe for Christianity," U.S. House of Representatives, March 28, 2006.

[150] Ron Paul, "US Shouldn't Cast Stones with Religious Persecution," *Texas Straight Talk*, Oct. 6, 1997.

[151] Ron Paul, "A New China Policy," U.S. House of Representatives, April 25, 2001.

[152] Ron Paul, "What the Price of Gold Is Telling Us," U.S. House of Representatives, April 25, 2006.

[153] Ron Paul, "The End of Dollar Hegemony," U.S. House of Representatives, Feb. 12, 2006.

[154] Ron Paul, "In the Name of Patriotism (Who Are the Patriots?)," U.S. House of Representatives, June 6, 2007.

[155] Ibid.

[156] Ron Paul, "Entangling Alliances," LewRockwell.com, Nov. 14, 2007.

[157] Ron Paul, "The Scandal at Walter Reed," U.S. House of Representatives, March 7, 2007.

[158] Ron Paul, "In the Name of Patriotism (Who Are the Patriots?)," U.S. House of Representatives, June 6, 2007.

[159] Ibid.

[160] Ron Paul, "Restricting the Executive Orders," *Texas Straight Talk*, Aug. 2, 1999.

[161] Ibid.

[162] Ron Paul, "Free Speech and Dietary Supplements," U.S. House of Representatives, Nov. 10, 2005.

[163] Ibid.

[164] Ibid.

[165] Ibid.

[166] Ron Paul, "Why Are Americans So Angry?" U.S. House of Representatives, June 29, 2006.

[167] Ibid.

[168] Ibid.

[169] Ibid.

[170] Ibid.

[171] Ibid.

[172] Ibid.

[173] Ron Paul, "Statement on HR 609, the 'Academic Bill of Rights'," U.S. House of Representatives, March 29, 2006.

[174] Ron Paul, "What Congress Can Do about Soaring Gas Prices," U.S. House of Representatives, May 2, 2006.

[175] Ibid.

[176] Ron Paul, "What the Price of Gold Is Telling Us," U.S. House of Representatives, April 25, 2006.

[177] Ibid.

[178] Ibid.

[179] Ibid.

[180] Ron Paul, "Statement for Hearing before the House Financial Services Committee, 'Monetary Policy and the State of the Economy'," U.S. House of Representatives, Feb. 15, 2007.

[181] Ibid.

[182] Ron Paul, "The End of Dollar Hegemony," U.S. House of Representatives, Feb. 12, 2006.

[183] Ron Paul, "Government Spending: A Tax on the Middle Class," U.S. House of Representatives, July 8, 2004.

[184] Ibid.

[185] Ron Paul, "Statement on HR 609, the 'Academic Bill of Rights'," U.S. House of Representatives, March 29, 2006.

[186] Ron Paul, "What the Price of Gold Is Telling Us," U.S. House of Representatives, April 25, 2006.

[187] Ibid.

[188] Ibid.

[189] Ron Paul, "Iran: The Next Neocon Target," U.S. House of Representatives, April 5, 2006.

[190] Ron Paul, "The End of Dollar Hegemony," U.S. House of Representatives, Feb. 12, 2006.

[191] Ron Paul, "Searching for a New Direction," U.S. House of Representatives, Jan. 18, 2006.

[192] Ron Paul, "Government Spending: A Tax on the Middle Class," U.S. House of Representatives, July 8, 2004.

[193] Ron Paul, "Statement before the Committee on Financial Services," U.S. House of Representatives, May 9, 2007.

[194] Ron Paul, "Staying or Leaving," U.S. House of Representatives, Oct. 7, 2005.

[195] Ron Paul, "Statement on So-Called 'Deficit Reduction Act'," U.S. House of Representatives, Nov. 18, 2005.

[196] Ron Paul, "Tax Cuts Benefit All Americans," *Texas Straight Talk,* Feb. 19, 2001.

[197] Kevin Landrigan, "Paul: Supporters Buying into Stance on Iraq," *The Telegraph,* Nov. 8, 2007.

[198] Ron Paul, "Reject the Millennium Challenge Act," U.S. House of Representatives, May 19, 2004.

[199] Ibid.

[200] Ibid.

[201] Ibid.

[202] Bill O'Reilly, Interview with Ron Paul, *The O'Reilly Factor,* Sept. 10, 2007.

[203] Ron Paul, "Why Are Americans So Angry?" U.S. House of Representatives, June 29, 2006.

[204] Ron Paul, "The Law of Opposites," U.S. House of Representatives, Sept. 7, 2006.

[205] Ibid.

[206] Ron Paul, "Iran: The Next Neocon Target," U.S. House of Representatives, April 5, 2006.

[207] Ron Paul, "We Have Been Warned," U.S. House of Representatives, Oct. 26, 2005.

[208] Ron Paul, "Staying or Leaving," U.S. House of Representatives, Oct. 7, 2005.

[209] Ron Paul, "What Does All This Mean?" U.S. House of Representatives, Sept. 8, 2005.

[210] Ibid.

[211] Ibid.

[212] Ron Paul, "The 9/11 Intelligence Bill: More Bureaucracy, More Intervention, Less Freedom," U.S. House of Representatives, Oct. 8, 2004.

[213] Ron Paul, "Entangling Alliances," LewRockwell.com, Nov. 14, 2007.

[214] Ron Paul, "Escalation Is Hardly the Answer," U.S. House of Representatives, Jan. 11, 2007.

[215] Ron Paul, "What the Price of Gold Is Telling Us," U.S. House of Representatives, April 25, 2006.

[216] Ron Paul, "Big Government Solutions Don't Work," U.S. House of Representatives, Sept. 7, 2006.

[217] Jon Stewart, Interview with Ron Paul, *The Daily Show*, June 4, 2007.

[218] Ron Paul, "Statement before the Financial Services Committee, Humphrey Hawkins Prequel Hearing," U.S. House of Representatives, July 17, 2007.

[219] Ron Paul, "Big Government Solutions Don't Work," U.S. House of Representatives, Sept. 7, 2006.

[220] Ron Paul, "IRS Threatens Political Speech," *Texas Straight Talk*, July 24, 2006.

[221] Ron Paul, "Big Government Solutions Don't Work," U.S. House of Representatives, Sept. 7, 2006.

[222] Ron Paul, "What Is Free Trade?" U.S. House of Representatives, May 2, 2000.

[223] Ibid.

[224] Ibid.

[225] Michael McCord, "Ron Paul's Constitutional Utopia," *Portsmouth Herald*, Nov. 18, 2007.

[226] Howard Fineman, "It's Independents' Day, In New Hampshire, Even Ron Paul Could Have a Shot," *Newsweek*, Oct. 27, 2007.

[227] Michael McCord, "Paul: Loss of Freedom Costly," Seacoastonline.com, Nov. 10, 2007.

[228] Ron Paul, "Security and Liberty," U.S. House of Representatives, April 25, 2007.

[229] Norma Love, "Paul Flush with Cash, Has Hopes for N.H.," *Guardian Unlimited*, Associated Press, Nov. 7, 2007.

[230] Ron Paul, "Why Are Americans So Angry?" U.S. House of Representatives, June 29, 2006.

[231] Ron Paul, "What Congress Can Do about Soaring Gas Prices," U.S. House of Representatives, May 2, 2006.

[232] Ibid.

[233] Ibid.

[234] Ron Paul, "What the Price of Gold Is Telling Us," U.S. House of Representatives, April 25, 2006.

[235] Ibid.

[236] Ibid.

[237] Ibid.

[238] Ibid.

[239] Ibid.

[240] Ibid.

[241] Ibid.

[242] Ibid.

[243] Ibid.

[244] Ibid.

[245] Ibid.

[246] Ibid.

[247] Ibid.

[248] Ibid.

[249] Ibid.

[250] Ibid.

[251] Ibid.

[252] Philip Haddad and Roger Marsh, Interview with Ron Paul, Pittsburgh Rally (Mars, PA), Aug. 3, 2007.

[253] Ron Paul, "The Coming Category 5 Financial Hurricane," U.S. House of Representatives, Sept. 15, 2005.

[254] Ron Paul, "The End of Dollar Hegemony," U.S. House of Representatives, Feb. 12, 2006.

[255] Mike Memoli, "Paul Talks Money, War in NH," MSNBC, Nov. 7, 2007.

[256] Ron Paul, "Why Are Americans So Angry?" U.S. House of Representatives, June 29, 2006.

[257] Ibid.

[258] Ron Paul, "Big Government Solutions Don't Work," U.S. House of Representatives, Sept. 7, 2006.

[259] Ibid.

[260] Ibid.

[261] Ron Paul, "The Law of Opposites," U.S. House of Representatives, Sept. 7, 2006.

[262] Ron Paul, "A Republic, If You Can Keep It," U.S. House of Representatives, Jan. 31 and Feb. 2, 2000.

[263] Ron Paul, "The Blame Game," U.S. House of Representatives, Dec. 7, 2005.

[264] Ron Paul, "Congress Erodes Privacy," U.S. House of Representatives, Nov. 16, 2005.

[265] Ron Paul, "Statement on the 'Sunlight Rule'," U.S. House of Representatives, March 3, 2006.

[266] Ron Paul, "Searching for a New Direction," U.S. House of Representatives, Jan. 18, 2006.

[267] Ibid.

[268] Ibid.

[269] Ibid.

[270] Ibid.

[271] Ibid.

[272] Ron Paul, "Where to from Here?" U.S. House of Representatives, Nov. 20, 2004.

[273] Ron Paul, "What the Price of Gold Is Telling Us," U.S. House of Representatives, April 25, 2006.

[274] Ron Paul, "Big Government Solutions Don't Work," U.S. House of Representatives, Sept. 7, 2006.

[275] Ron Paul, "What the Price of Gold Is Telling Us," U.S. House of Representatives, April 25, 2006.

[276] Ron Paul, "The Law of Opposites," U.S. House of Representatives, Sept. 7, 2006.

[277] Ibid.

[278] Ron Paul, "Congress Erodes Privacy," U.S. House of Representatives, Nov. 16, 2005.

[279] Ron Paul, "Statement on Counter-Terrorism Proposals and Civil Liberties," U.S. House of Representatives, Oct. 12, 2001.

[280] Ibid.

[281] Ron Paul, "A Tribute to the Late Harry Browne," U.S. House of Representatives, March 30, 2006.

[282] Ron Paul, "Unconstitutional Legislation Threatens Freedoms," U.S. House of Representatives, May 7, 2007.

[283] Ron Paul, "Statement before the Joint Economic Committee," U.S. House of Representatives, Nov. 8, 2007.

[284] Ron Paul, "What the Price of Gold Is Telling Us," U.S. House of Representatives, April 25, 2006.

[285] Ron Paul, "Statement on Immigration Agreement," U.S. House of Representatives, May 18, 2007.

[286] Ron Paul, "Immigration and the Welfare State," *Texas Straight Talk*, Aug. 8, 2005.

[287] Ron Paul, "Don't Complicate Immigration Reform," *Texas Straight Talk*, Dec. 12, 2005.

[288] Ibid.

[289] Ron Paul, "A Republic, If You Can Keep It," U.S. House of Representatives, Jan. 31 and Feb. 2, 2000.

[290] Ron Paul, "What the Price of Gold Is Telling Us," U.S. House of Representatives, April 25, 2006.

[291] Ibid.

[292] Ibid.

[293] Ibid.

[294] Ron Paul, "Iran: The Next Neocon Target," U.S. House of Representatives, April 5, 2006.

[295] Ron Paul, "The Coming Category 5 Financial Hurricane," U.S. House of Representatives, Sept. 15, 2005.

[296] Ibid.

[297] Ibid.

[298] Ibid.

[299] Ron Paul, "What the Price of Gold Is Telling Us," U.S. House of Representatives, April 25, 2006.

[300] Ron Paul, "Opening Statement Committee on Financial Services Paulson Hearing," U.S. House of Representatives, June 20, 2007.

[301] Ron Paul, "The Republican Congress Wastes Billions Overseas," U.S. House of Representatives, July 20, 2005.

[302] Ron Paul, "Opposition to HR 552," U.S. House of Representatives, Sept. 4, 2007.

[303] Ron Paul, "Iran: The Next Neocon Target," U.S. House of Representatives, April 5, 2006.

[304] Ibid.

[305] Ron Paul, "The Law of Opposites," U.S. House of Representatives, Sept. 7, 2006.

[306] Ibid.

[307] Ron Paul, "The Scandal at Walter Reed," U.S. House of Representatives, March 7, 2007.

[308] Ibid.

[309] Ibid.

[310] Ibid.

[311] Ron Paul, "Making the World Safe for Christianity," U.S. House of Representatives, March 28, 2006.

[312] Ron Paul, "Iran: The Next Neocon Target," U.S. House of Representatives, April 5, 2006.

[313] Ibid.

[314] Ron Paul, "The Law of Opposites," U.S. House of Representatives, Sept. 7, 2006.

[315] Ibid.

[316] Ibid.

[317] Ibid.

[318] Ron Paul, "Don't Do It, Mr. President," U.S. House of Representatives, Feb. 6, 2007.

[319] Ron Paul, "Statement on H Con Res 21," U.S. House of Representatives, June 20, 2007.

[320] Ibid.

[321] Ron Paul, "Iran: The Next Neocon Target," U.S. House of Representatives, April 5, 2006.

[322] Ibid.

[323] Ibid.

[324] Ibid.

[325] Ibid.

[326] Ibid.

[327] Ron Paul, "Don't Do It, Mr. President," U.S. House of Representatives, Feb. 6, 2007.

[328] Ibid.

[329] Ibid.

[330] Ibid.

[331] Ibid.

[332] Ibid.

[333] Ibid.

[334] Ron Paul, "Why Are Americans So Angry?" U.S. House of Representatives, June 29, 2006.

[335] Ron Paul, "The Law of Opposites," U.S. House of Representatives, Sept. 7, 2006.

[336] Ibid.

[337] Ibid.

[338] Ibid.

[339] Ibid.

[340] Ibid.

[341] Ron Paul, "Escalation Is Hardly the Answer," U.S. House of Representatives, Jan. 11, 2007.

[342] James Q. Lynch, "Response to Message Impresses Paul," *The Gazette*, Nov. 17, 2007.

[343] Ron Paul, "What Congress Can Do about Soaring Gas Prices," U.S. House of Representatives, May 2, 2006.

[344] Ron Paul, "Iran: The Next Neocon Target," U.S. House of Representatives, April 5, 2006.

[345] Ron Paul, "Why Are Americans So Angry?" U.S. House of Representatives, June 29, 2006.

[346] Ron Paul, "Everybody Supports the Troops," U.S. House of Representatives, Jan. 18, 2007.

[347] Ron Paul, "Statement on the Iraq War Resolution," U.S. House of Representatives, Feb. 14, 2007.

[348] Ron Paul, "The Upcoming Iraq War Funding Bill," U.S. House of Representatives, March 20, 2007.

[349] Ibid.

[350] Ibid.

[351] Ibid.

[352] Ibid.

[353] Ibid.

[354] Ron Paul, "We Just Marched In (So We Can Just March Out)," U.S. House of Representatives, April 17, 2007.

[355] Ibid.

[356] Ibid.

[357] Ibid.

[358] Ibid.

[359] Ibid.

[360] Ron Paul, "Statement on HR 2956, the Responsible Redeployment from Iraq Act," U.S. House of Representatives, July 12, 2007.

[361] Ron Paul, "Statement on HR 3159, the Ensuring Military Readiness through Stability and Predictability Deployment Policy Act," U.S. House of Representatives, Aug. 2, 2007.

[362] Ron Paul, "The Blame Game," U.S. House of Representatives, Dec. 7, 2005.

[363] Ibid.

[364] Ibid.

[365] Ibid.

[366] Ibid.

[367] Ron Paul, "Big Lies and Little Lies," U.S. House of Representatives, Nov. 2, 2005.

[368] Ron Paul, "Staying or Leaving," U.S. House of Representatives, Oct. 7, 2005.

[369] Ibid.

[370] Ron Paul, "Why We Fight," U.S. House of Representatives, Sept. 8, 2005.

[371] Ron Paul, "Why We Fight," U.S. House of Representatives, Sept. 8, 2005.

[372] Ibid.

[373] Ron Paul, "What Does All This Mean?" U.S. House of Representatives, Sept. 8, 2005.

[374] Ron Paul, "The Law of Opposites," U.S. House of Representatives, Sept. 7, 2006.

[375] Ron Paul, "Wagging Imperialism as Bad as the Dog," *Texas Straight Talk*, Aug. 24, 1998.

[376] Ibid.

[377] Ron Paul, "Why We Should Not Fight," U.S. House of Representatives," Sept. 8, 2005.

[378] Ron Paul, "Making the World Safe for Christianity," U.S. House of Representatives, March 28, 2006.

[379] Ron Paul, "The Law of Opposites," U.S. House of Representatives, Sept. 7, 2006.

[380] Ibid.

[381] Ron Paul, "Why We Fight," U.S. House of Representatives, Sept. 8, 2005.

[382] Ron Paul, "Why We Should Not Fight," U.S. House of Representatives, Sept. 8, 2005.

[383] Ron Paul, "The Blame Game," U.S. House of Representatives, Dec. 7, 2005.

[384] Ron Paul, "What the Price of Gold Is Telling Us," U.S. House of Representatives, April 25, 2006.

[385] Tucker Carlson, MSNBC, Interview with Ron Paul, June 6, 2007.

[386] Ron Paul, "Big Government Solutions Don't Work," U.S. House of Representatives, Sept. 7, 2006.

[387] Ron Paul, "The 9/11 Intelligence Bill: More Bureaucracy, More Intervention, Less Freedom," U.S. House of Representatives, Oct. 8, 2004.

[388] Ron Paul, "Reject Draft Slavery," U.S. House of Representatives, Oct. 5, 2004.

[389] Ron Paul, "Statement on H.Res 648," U.S. House of Representatives, Feb. 1, 2006.

[390] Ron Paul, "Statement on H.Res 648," U.S. House of Representatives, Feb. 1, 2006.

[391] Ibid.

[392] Ron Paul, "Searching for a New Direction," U.S. House of Representatives, Jan. 18, 2006.

[393] Ibid.

[394] Ron Paul, "Searching for a New Direction," U.S. House of Representatives, Jan. 18, 2006.

[395] Ron Paul, "In the Name of Patriotism (Who Are the Patriots?)," U.S. House of Representatives, June 6, 2007.

[396] Ron Paul, "Is America a Police State?" U.S. House of Representatives, June 27, 2002.

[397] Ron Paul, "Big Government Solutions Don't Work," U.S. House of Representatives, Sept. 7, 2006.

[398] Ron Paul, "Campaign Finance Reform," *Texas Straight Talk*, April 9, 2001.

[399] Ron Paul, "IRS Church Seizure Is a Tragedy for Religious Liberty," *Texas Straight Talk*, Feb. 26, 2001.

[400] Ron Paul, "'Campaign Finance Reform Muzzles Political Dissent," U.S. House of Representatives, Dec. 22, 2003.

[401] Ron Paul, "Reject a National Prescription Database," U.S. House of Representatives, Oct. 5, 2004.

[402] Ibid.

[403] Ibid.

[404] Ron Paul, "Iran: The Next Neocon Target," U.S. House of Representatives, April 5, 2006.

[405] Ron Paul, "The Law of Opposites," U.S. House of Representatives, Sept. 7, 2006.

[406] Ibid.

[407] Ibid.

[408] Ron Paul, "The Law of Opposites," U.S. House of Representatives, Sept. 7, 2006.

[409] Ibid.

[410] Ibid.

[411] Ron Paul, "Iran: The Next Neocon Target," U.S. House of Representatives, April 5, 2006.

[412] Ron Paul, "A Republic, If You Can Keep It," U.S. House of Representatives, Jan. 31 and Feb. 2, 2000.

[413] Daymond Steer, "Ron Quixote," The Cabinet, Small Town Papers News Service, Nov. 16, 2007.

[414] Ron Paul, "Patriotism," U.S. House of Representatives, May 22, 2007.

[415] Ibid.

[416] Ibid.

[417] Ron Paul, "Staying or Leaving," U.S. House of Representatives, Oct. 7, 2005.

[418] Ron Paul, "Crazed Foreign Aid," U.S House of Representatives, Oct. 17, 2003.

[419] Ibid.

[420] Ibid.

[421] Ron Paul, "Escalation Is Hardly the Answer," U.S. House of Representatives, Jan. 11, 2007.

[422] Ibid.

[423] Ron Paul, "Neo Conned," U.S. House of Representatives, July 10, 2003.

[424] Ron Paul, "Minimum Wage Increase Act," U.S. House of Representatives, March 9, 2000.

[425] Ibid.

[426] Ron Paul, "Opening Statement Committee on Financial Services, Paulson Hearing," U.S. House of Representatives, June 20, 2007.

[427] Ron Paul, "Why We Fight," U.S. House of Representatives, Sept. 8, 2005.

[428] Ron Paul, "Keep Your Eye on the Target," U.S. House of Representatives, Nov. 29, 2001.

[429] Ibid.

[430] Ron Paul, "Paper Money and Tyranny," U.S. House of Representatives, Sept. 5, 2003.

[431] Ron Paul, Speech, U.S. House of Representatives, June 13, 2007.

[432] Ron Paul, "The Blame Game," U.S. House of Representatives, Dec. 7, 2005.

[433] Ron Paul, "In the Name of Patriotism (Who Are the Patriots?)," U.S. House of Representatives, June 6, 2007.

[434] Ron Paul, "The 9/11 Intelligence Bill: More Bureaucracy, More Intervention, Less Freedom," U.S. House of Representatives, Oct. 8, 2004.

[435] Ibid.

[436] Ron Paul, "Why Are Americans So Angry?" U.S. House of Representatives, June 29, 2006.

[437] Ron Paul, "Iran: The Next Neocon Target," U.S. House of Representatives, April 5, 2006.

[438] Ibid.

[439] Ron Paul, "Making the World Safe for Christianity," U.S. House of Representatives, March 28, 2006.

[440] Ibid.

[441] Ron Paul, "Why We Fight," U.S. House of Representatives, Sept. 8, 2005.

[442] Ron Paul, "The Crucial Moral Issue: Respect for Life," U.S. House of Representatives, Nov. 20, 2004.

[443] Ron Paul, "The Law of Opposites," U.S. House of Representatives, Sept. 7, 2006.

[444] Ron Paul, "Iran: The Next Neocon Target," U.S. House of Representatives, April 5, 2006.

[445] Ibid.

[446] Ibid.

[447] Ron Paul, "Statement on the Iraq War Resolution," U.S. House of Representatives, Feb. 14, 2007.

[448] Ron Paul, "Staying or Leaving," U.S. House of Representatives, Oct. 7, 2005.

[449] Ron Paul, "Questions That Won't Be Asked about Iraq," U.S. House of Representatives, Sept. 10, 2002.

[450] Ron Paul, Speech, U.S. House of Representatives, Sept. 25, 2001.

[451] Ron Paul, "Entangling Alliances," LewRockwell.com, Nov. 14, 2007.

452 Ibid.

453 Ibid.

454 Ron Paul, "Big Government Solutions Don't Work," U.S. House of Representatives, Sept. 7, 2006.

455 Ron Paul, "Introduction of the Teacher Tax Cut Act," U.S. House of Representatives, Jan. 31, 2001.

456 Ron Paul, "Keeping Promises about Social Security," *Texas Straight Talk*, Feb. 14, 2000.

457 Ron Paul, "In the Name of Patriotism (Who Are the Patriots?)," U.S. House of Representatives, June 6, 2007.

458 Ibid.

459 Ron Paul, "Congress Erodes Privacy," U.S. House of Representatives, Nov. 16, 2005.

460 Laura Knoy, Ron Paul Interview, NHPR, June 5, 2007.

461 Ron Paul, "Why Are Americans So Angry?" U.S. House of Representatives, June 29, 2006.

462 Ron Paul, "In the Name of Patriotism (Who Are the Patriots?)," U.S. House of Representatives, June 6, 2007.

463 Ibid.

464 Ibid.

465 Ibid.

466 Ibid.

467 Ibid.

468 Ibid.

469 Ron Paul, "Honoring Phil Crane," U.S. House of Representatives, Nov. 17, 2004.

470 Ibid.

471 Ron Paul, "Federal Courts and the Pledge of Allegiance," U.S. House of Representatives, Sept. 23, 2004.

472 Ibid.

473 Ibid.

[474] Ibid.

[475] Michael Hampton, "Ron Paul Grassroots Support Proved," HomelandSecurity.com, Feb. 25, 2007.

[476] Ron Paul, "What Does All This Mean?" U.S. House of Representatives, Sept. 8, 2005.

[477] Ron Paul, "The Terrible Cost of Government," *Texas Straight Talk*, July 28, 2003.

[478] Ron Paul, "Statement before the Financial Services Committee, Humphrey Hawkins Prequel Hearing," U.S. House of Representatives, July 17, 2007.

[479] Ron Paul, "Iran: The Next Neocon Target," U.S. House of Representatives, April 5, 2006.

[480] Ron Paul, "Free Trade Rhetoric Often Obscures Agenda," *Texas Straight Talk*, March 22, 1999.

[481] Ron Paul, "Steel Tariffs Are Taxes on American Consumers," *Texas Straight Talk*, March 18, 2002.

[482] Ibid.

[483] Ron Paul, "In the Name of Patriotism (Who Are the Patriots?)," U.S. House of Representatives, June 6, 2007.

[484] Ron Paul, "Police State USA," *Texas Straight Talk*, Aug. 9, 2004.

[485] Ron Paul, "In the Name of Patriotism (Who Are the Patriots?)," U.S. House of Representatives, June 6, 2007.

[486] Ron Paul, "Can Freedom Be Exchanged for Security?" *Texas Straight Talk*, Nov. 26, 2001.

[487] Ron Paul, "Government and Racism," U.S. House of Representatives, Feb. 16, 2007.

[488] Ron Paul, "The End of Dollar Hegemony," U.S. House of Representatives, Feb. 12, 2006.

[489] Ron Paul, "The Same Old Failed Policies in Iraq," U.S. House of Representatives, June 3, 2004.

[490] Ron Paul, "Inspection or Invasion in Iraq?" U.S. House of Representatives, June 24, 2002.

[491] Ron Paul, "The Unbearable Cost of Running Iraq," *Texas Straight Talk*, June 9, 2003.

[492] Ron Paul, "A Republic, If You Can Keep It," U.S. House of Representatives, Jan. 31 and Feb. 2, 2000.

[493] Ibid.

[494] Ibid.

[495] Ron Paul, "The Crucial Moral Issue: Respect for Life," U.S. House of Representatives, Nov. 20, 2004.

[496] Ron Paul, "Partial-Birth Abortion Ban Act of 2000," U.S. House of Representatives, April 5, 2000.

[497] Ron Paul, "Stem Cell Research and Human Cloning," U.S. House of Representatives, July 31, 2001.

[498] Ron Paul, "Where to from Here?" U.S. House of Representatives, Nov. 20, 2004.

[499] Jon Stewart, Interview with Ron Paul, *The Daily Show*, June 4, 2007.

[500] O. Kay Henderson, "Five Candidates in Iowa over Weekend," *Radio Iowa News*, Nov. 18, 2007.

[501] Mark Davis, "Paul's Promise: Less Government," *Valley News*, Nov. 15, 2007.

[502] John Deeth, "The Revolution at the Tailgates: Ron Paul," *Iowa Independent*, Nov. 17, 2007.

[503] Wolf, Z. Byron, "Ron Paul: Republican or Revolutionary?" *ABC News*, Oct. 18, 2007.

[504] Molly Hottle, "Paul Wants to Limit Government on Taxes, Foreign Policy," *Des Moines Register*, Oct. 28, 2007.

[505] Ron Paul, "Staying or Leaving," U.S. House of Representatives, Oct. 7, 2005.

[506] GOP Presidential Debate, Columbia, SC, *Fox News*, May 2007.

[507] Ron Paul, "Dialogue Is Key to Dealing with Iran," U.S. House of Representatives, June 20, 2006.

[508] Michael Smerconish, "Swooning (Just a Bit) for Ron Paul," *Philadelphia Daily News*, Nov. 15, 2007.

[509] Ron Paul, "3000 American Deaths in Iraq," U.S. House of Representatives, Jan. 5, 2007.

[510] Ron Paul, "The Blame Game," U.S. House of Representatives, Dec. 7, 2005.

[511] Ron Paul, "Big Lies and Little Lies," U.S. House of Representatives, Nov. 2, 2005.

[512] Ron Paul, "Why We Fight," U.S. House of Representatives, Sept. 8, 2005.

[513] Ron Paul, "Statement of Congressman Paul on HR 180," U.S. House of Representatives, July 30, 2007.

[514] Ron Paul, "Restoring the Second Amendment," U.S. House of Representatives, Jan. 9, 2003.

[515] Ibid.

[516] Ibid.

[517] Ron Paul, "Assault Weapons and Assaults on the Constitution," *Texas Straight Talk*, April 21, 2003.

[518] Ibid.

[519] Ibid.

[520] Ibid.

[521] Ibid.

[522] Ron Paul, "Is America a Police State?" U.S. House of Representatives, June 27, 2002.

[523] Ibid.

[524] Ibid.

[525] Ibid.

[526] Ibid.

[527] Ibid.

[528] Ibid.

[529] Ibid.

[530] Jay Root, "Rep. Ron Paul Does It His Way," *The Kansas City Star*, Nov. 14, 2007.

[531] Ron Paul, "The Crucial Moral Issue: Respect for Life," U.S. House of Representatives, Nov. 20, 2004.

[532] Charles Babington, "Ron Paul Finds Fans, Funds on the Fringe," Associated Press, Nov. 15, 2007.

[533] Ron Paul, "Keeping Promises about Social Security," *Texas Straight Talk*, Feb. 14, 2000.

[534] Ibid.

[535] Ibid.

[536] Ibid.

[537] Ron Paul, "What the Price of Gold Is Telling Us," U.S. House of Representatives, April 25, 2006.

[538] Ibid.

[539] Ibid.

[540] Ibid.

[541] Ron Paul, "Praising Private Space Exploration," U.S. House of Representatives, June 25, 2004.

[542] Ibid.

[543] Ibid.

[544] Ibid.

[545] Ibid.

[546] Ron Paul, "Big Government Solutions Don't Work," U.S. House of Representatives, Sept. 7, 2006.

[547] Ron Paul, "Statement on the Iraq War Resolution," U.S. House of Representatives, Feb. 14, 2007.

[548] Ron Paul, "Searching for a New Direction," U.S. House of Representatives, Jan. 18, 2006.

[549] Ron Paul, "What the Price of Gold Is Telling Us," U.S. House of Representatives, April 25, 2006.

[550] Ron Paul, "Big Government Solutions Don't Work," U.S. House of Representatives, Sept. 7, 2006.

[551] Ron Paul, "The Coming Category 5 Financial Hurricane," U.S. House of Representatives, Sept. 15, 2005.

[552] Ibid.

[553] Ron Paul, "Where to from Here?" U.S. House of Representatives, Nov. 20, 2004.

[554] Ron Paul, "Raising the Debt Limit: A Disgrace," U.S. House of Representatives, Nov. 18, 2004.

[555] Ibid.

[556] Ibid.

[557] Ron Paul, "Government Spending: A Tax on the Middle Class," U.S. House of Representatives, July 8, 2004.

[558] Ron Paul, "The Scandal at Walter Reed," U.S. House of Representatives, March 7, 2007.

[559] Ron Paul, "Federal Courts and the Pledge of Allegiance," U.S. House of Representatives, Sept. 23, 2004.

[560] Ibid.

[561] Ibid.

[562] Ron Paul, "In the Name of Patriotism (Who Are the Patriots?)," U.S. House of Representatives, June 6, 2007.

[563] Ibid.

[564] Ron Paul, "After 222 Years Liberty Must Still Be Our Goal," *Texas Straight Talk*, June 29, 1998.

[565] Ron Paul, "Waco: The Smoking Gun," *Texas Straight Talk*, Sept. 6, 1999.

[566] Ron Paul, "What the Price of Gold Is Telling Us," U.S. House of Representatives, April 25, 2006.

[567] Ron Paul, "Hands Off Sudan!" U.S. House of Representatives, July 23, 2004.

[568] Ibid.

[569] Ron Paul, "Intervention in Sudan," U.S. House of Representatives, June 13, 2001.

[570] Ibid.

[571] Ron Paul, "The Scandal at Walter Reed," U.S. House of Representatives, March 7, 2007.

[572] Ron Paul, "Why Are Americans So Angry?" U.S. House of Representatives, June 29, 2006.

[573] Ron Paul, "Domestic Surveillance and the Patriot Act," *Texas Straight Talk*, Dec. 26, 2005.

[574] Ron Paul, "Stopping the Surveillance State," *Texas Straight Talk*, Jan. 18, 1999.

[575] Ron Paul, "Statement of Ron Paul on the Freedom and Privacy Restoration Act (HR 220)," U.S. House of Representatives, May 18, 2000.

[576] Ron Paul, "We Have Been Warned," U.S. House of Representatives, Oct. 26, 2005.

[577] Ibid.

[578] Ibid.

[579] Ibid.

[580] Ibid.

[581] Ron Paul, "Big Government Solutions Don't Work," U.S. House of Representatives, Sept. 7, 2006.

[582] Ron Paul, "A Republic, If You Can Keep It," U.S. House of Representatives, Jan. 31 and Feb. 2, 2000.

[583] Jay Leno, Interview with Ron Paul, *The Tonight Show with Jay Leno,* Oct. 30, 2007.

[584] Ron Paul, "Statement on the Iraq War Resolution," U.S. House of Representatives, Feb. 14, 2007.

[585] Jon Stewart, Interview with Ron Paul, *The Daily Show,* June 4, 2007.

[586] Super Tuesday MSNBC, Interview with Ron Paul, Sept. 25, 2007.

[587] Ron Paul, "Candidate Central, Ron Paul," *Forbes,* Oct. 2, 2007.

[588] Ron Paul, "What Is Free Trade," U.S. House of Representatives, May 2, 2000.

[589] Amanda Kathryn Hydro and Jason Mercier, "Time to Shine Light on Government Spending," *Fox News,* Oct. 23, 2007.

[590] Ron Paul, "Statement for Hearing before the House Financial Services Committee, 'Monetary Policy and the State of the Economy'," U.S. House of Representatives, Feb. 15, 2007.

[591] Ron Paul, "Opening Statement Committee on Financial Services, Paulson Hearing," U.S. House of Representatives, June 20, 2007.

[592] Ibid.

[593] Ron Paul, "Statement on HR 2956, the Responsible Redeployment from Iraq Act," U.S. House of Representatives, July 12, 2007.

[594] Ron Paul, "Statement on HR 3159, Ensuring Military Readiness," U.S. House of Representatives, Aug. 2, 2007.

[595] Ron Paul, "More of the Same in 2007," *Texas Straight Talk,* Dec. 25, 2006.

[596] Ron Paul, "Dialogue Is Key to Dealing with Iran," U.S. House of Representatives, June 20, 2006.

[597] Ron Paul, "Statement on H Con Res 21," U.S. House of Representatives, June 20, 2007.

[598] Ron Paul, "We Have Been Warned," U.S. House of Representatives, Oct. 26, 2005.

[599] Ron Paul, "Staying or Leaving," U.S. House of Representatives, Oct. 7, 2005.

[600] Ron Paul, "Where to from Here?" U.S. House of Representatives, Nov. 20, 2004

[601] Ron Paul, Speech, U.S. House of Representatives, Sept. 25, 2001.

[602] Ron Paul, "Staying or Leaving," U.S. House of Representatives, Oct. 7, 2005.

[603] Ron Paul, "What Does All This Mean?" U.S. House of Representatives, Sept. 8, 2005.

[604] Jay Leno, Interview with Ron Paul, *The Tonight Show with Jay Leno,* Oct. 30, 2007.

[605] Larry Fester, "Ron Paul Brings His 'Freedom Revolution' to Independence Hall," *USA Daily,* Nov. 10, 2007.

[606] Ron Paul, "What the Price of Gold Is Telling Us," U.S. House of Representatives, April 25, 2006.

[607] Ron Paul, "Iran: The Next Neocon Target," U.S. House of Representatives, April 5, 2006.

[608] Ron Paul, "Why Are Americans So Angry?" U.S. House of Representatives, June 29, 2006.

[609] Ron Paul, "Big Government Solutions Don't Work," U.S. House of Representatives, Sept. 7, 2006.

[610] Ron Paul, "The Law of Opposites," U.S. House of Representatives, Sept. 7, 2006.

[611] Ron Paul, "In the Name of Patriotism (Who Are the Patriots?)," U.S. House of Representatives, June 6, 2007.

[612] Ron Paul, "Iran: The Next Neocon Target," U.S. House of Representatives, April 5, 2006.

[613] Ron Paul, "The Blame Game," U.S. House of Representatives, Dec. 7, 2005.

[614] Ron Paul, "The End of Dollar Hegemony," U.S. House of Representatives, Feb. 12, 2006.

[615] Ron Paul, "What Does All This Mean?" U.S. House of Representatives, Sept. 8, 2005.

[616] Ron Paul, "The Crucial Moral Issue: Respect for Life," U.S. House of Representatives, Nov. 20, 2004.

[617] Ron Paul, "Reject Draft Slavery," U.S. House of Representatives, Oct. 5, 2004.

[618] Ron Paul, "In the Name of Patriotism (Who Are the Patriots?)," U.S. House of Representatives, June 6, 2007.

[619] Ron Paul, "Reject a National Prescription Database," U.S. House of Representatives, Oct. 5, 2004.

[620] Ibid.

[621] Ron Paul, "A Wise Consistency," U.S. House of Representatives, Feb. 11, 2004.

[622] Ibid.

[623] Ron Paul, "Why Are Americans So Angry?" U.S. House of Representatives, June 29, 2006.

[624] Ron Paul, "The Law of Opposites," U.S. House of Representatives, Sept. 7, 2006.

[625] Ron Paul, "Statement on the Iraq War Resolution," U.S. House of Representatives, Feb. 14, 2007.

[626] Ron Paul, "Iran: The Next Neocon Target," U.S. House of Representatives, April 5, 2006.

[627] Ron Paul, "The 9/11 Intelligence Bill: More Bureaucracy, More Intervention, Less Freedom," U.S. House of Representatives, Oct. 8, 2004.

[628] Ibid.

[629] Ron Paul, "Why Are Americans So Angry?" U.S. House of Representatives, June 29, 2006.

[630] Ibid.

[631] Ron Paul, "3000 American Deaths in Iraq," U.S. House of Representatives, Jan. 5, 2007.

[632] Ron Paul, "War Profiteers," LewRockwell.com, April 9, 2003.

[633] Ron Paul, "Iran: The Next Neocon Target," U.S. House of Representatives, April 5, 2006.

[634] Ron Paul, "Why Are Americans So Angry?" U.S. House of Representatives, June 29, 2006.

[635] Ron Paul, "The End of Dollar Hegemony," U.S. House of Representatives, Feb. 12, 2006.

[636] Ron Paul, "A Wise Consistency," U.S. House of Representatives, Feb. 11, 2004.

[637] Ron Paul, "What the Price of Gold Is Telling Us," U.S. House of Representatives, April 25, 2006.

[638] Ron Paul, "The End of Dollar Hegemony," U.S. House of Representatives, Feb. 12, 2006.

[639] Ibid.

[640] Ron Paul, "Why We Should Not Fight," U.S. House of Representatives, Sept. 8, 2005.

[641] Ron Paul, "Why Are Americans So Angry?" U.S. House of Representatives, June 29, 2006.

[642] Ron Paul, "Big Government Solutions Don't Work," U.S. House of Representatives, Sept. 7, 2006.

[643] Ibid.

[644] Ron Paul, "Statement for Hearing before the House Financial Services Committee, 'Monetary Policy and the State of the Economy'," U.S. House of Representatives, Feb. 15, 2007.

[645] Ron Paul, "Tax Cuts and Class Wars," *Texas Straight Talk*, Jan. 20, 2003.

[646] Ron Paul, "A Republic, If You Can Keep It," U.S. House of Representatives, Jan. 31 and Feb. 2, 2000.

[647] Ibid.

[648] Ron Paul, "The Blame Game," U.S. House of Representatives, Dec. 7, 2005.

[649] Ron Paul, "Why We Should Not Fight," U.S. House of Representatives, Sept. 8, 2005.

[650] Ron Paul, "A Wise Consistency," U.S. House of Representatives, Feb. 11, 2004.

[651] Ron Paul, "Opening Statement Committee on Financial Services, World Bank Hearing," U.S. House of Representatives, May 22, 2007.

[652] Ibid.

[653] Ibid.

[654] Ibid.

[655] Lisa Anderson, "Paul: A Seller of Ideas," *Chicago Tribune*, Nov. 13, 2007.

[656] Brian Farmer, "Interview with Ron Paul," *The New American*, Oct. 1, 2007.

About the Editors

PHILIP HADDAD is pursuing a degree in political science. He is a political columnist with the southwestern Pennsylvania regional magazine, *Curb*. As an actor, he has been involved in regional theater. He recently appeared as the lead male role in the independent film, *Mars Attacks Mt. Pleasant*, now in post-production. Haddad lives in Scottdale, Pennsylvania.

ROGER MARSH is a content producer who has worked as a writer, playwright, Web producer, and independent filmmaker. Ten of his plays have been produced–all works of comedy, including his serial dramedy, *Dime Novel Radio Theater*. As an acquisitions editor for major book publishers, hundreds of his book projects have been distributed both domestically and internationally, including the quote books, *Wit & Wisdom of Baseball* and *Wit & Wisdom of Golf*, and *The New York Times* best seller, *Ross Perot: What Does He Stand For?* He is the coauthor of *Julie Taymor: Art on Stage and Screen,* and his first film, *Haunted R&R Station,* was released on DVD in June 2006. He wrote and directed the full-length comedy, *Mars Attacks Mt. Pleasant,* which will be released in 2008. Marsh lives in Chicago with his wife, Joyce, and daughter, Laine.